Praise for *The Six Fundamentals of Success*

"Strategic advantage will go to companies that get the fundamentals right. This book lays out what anyone needs to know to win in business today."
—Richard Silverman, Vice Chairman, Fleet National Bank

"Any ambitious, thoughtful, and upwardly mobile manager should find many useful, career-enhancing pointers in *The Six Fundamentals of Success*."
—Josh S. Weston, former CEO, Automatic Data Processing Inc.

"The fundamentals and rules in this book created the foundation for the accelerated learning of our senior leadership team and subsequently our entire organization . . . they helped us to focus on the customer, eliminate communication breakdowns, and strengthen our financial performance."
—Thomas J. McAteer, Jr., President and CEO,
Vytra Health Plans

"Levine's fundamentals—adding value, communicating, having the discipline to get the job done, working with integrity, investing in relationships, and gaining perspective are global concepts that cross all boundaries."
—Clark Winter, Chief Global Investment Strategist,
The Citigroup Private Bank

"Clear, concise common sense. The most valuable business book in years."
—Matthew T. Crosson, President,
Long Island Association, Inc.

"Companies have to execute better, get more out of less, and make fewer mistakes. They need to focus on the business issues that make a difference. Levine's book shows the perfect ways to do this."
—John Kanas, Chairman, President, and CEO,
North Fork Bank

"Stuart Levine's life-long commitment to learning, to building strong cultures, and to focusing on values are expertly represented in this book. A must-read for all those who care."
—Michael J. Dowling, President and CEO, North Shore–LIJ Health System

"While there are no quick fixes, *The Six Fundamentals of Success* is a great book for a leader who's stretched thin and wants to let his or her team know how to get things right. I love this book!"
—James Orsini, Group Chief Financial Officer, Interbrand Corporation

"*The Six Fundamentals of Success* gets everyone working toward the same goals to achieve the desired results. The book shows how to lead a team, be on a team, and how to energize the team!"
—Jack Leahy, Managing Director, The Citigroup Private Bank

"This book provides an extraordinary opportunity for people at all levels to develop and strengthen their leadership skills."
—Ronald A. Malone, Chairman and CEO, Gentiva Health Services

"'Don't let others define you' is but one of the many powerful rules from this book. Every reader will take away something different, but whatever it is, it will make an impact on your business career and your life."
—Larry Tarica, President, Jimlar Corporation

"Stuart Levine provides tremendous value with his targeted messages. This book is another example of his relentless focus on the customer."
—Margaret T. Watkins, President, Meritas

THE SIX
FUNDAMENTALS
OF SUCCESS

THE SIX
FUNDAMENTALS
OF SUCCESS

THE RULES FOR GETTING IT RIGHT
FOR YOURSELF AND YOUR ORGANIZATION

STUART R. LEVINE

CURRENCY   DOUBLEDAY

NEW YORK   LONDON   TORONTO   SYDNEY   AUCKLAND

A CURRENCY BOOK
PUBLISHED BY DOUBLEDAY
a division of Random House, Inc.

CURRENCY is a trademark of Random House, Inc., and DOUBLEDAY is
a registered trademark of Random House, Inc.

Book design by Elizabeth Rendfleisch

Library of Congress Cataloging-in-Publication Data
Levine, Stuart R.
The six fundamentals of success : the rules for getting it right for
yourself and your organization / Stuart R. Levine.— 1st US ed.
p.   cm.
"A Currency book."
1. Industrial management. 2. Organizational behavior. 3. Psychology,
Industrial. 4. Interpersonal relations. 5. Interpersonal
communication. 6. Customer relations. 7. Success in business.
I. Title.
HD31.L3847 2004
658—dc22   2003060768

ISBN 0-385-51086-1

PRINTED IN THE UNITED STATES OF AMERICA

First United States Edition: January 2004

SPECIAL SALES
Currency Books are available at special discounts for bulk purchases
for sales promotions or premiums. Special editions, including
personalized covers, excerpts of existing books, and corporate
imprints, can be created in large quantities for special needs. For more
information, write to Special Markets, Currency Books,
specialmarkets@randomhouse.com

3   5   7   9   10   8   6   4

To Harriet—it's a privilege to share my
business, life, and love with you.

To Jesse and Elizabeth
For your support—your growth provides
a constant source of joy and pride.

CONTENTS

Fundamental #2 · Communicate Up and Down, Inside and Out

ACKNOWLEDGMENTS

Thanks to my literary agent, Martha Jewett, and to Anne Cole and Roger Scholl of Doubleday for their extraordinary skill and commitment. Also, I want to thank Sally Allen for bringing a fantastic learning energy to the book process and for her relentless dedication to getting it right for the reader. Larry Tarica's ongoing contribution to this book defines friendship.

This book reflects the insight, intelligence, and passion of the following people who shared their business and life experience with me and my team and sustained us throughout its development: Tom Allen, Mark B. Anderson, Ton J. de Boer, Michael J. Dowling, Brendan Dugan, Kerry Edwards, Russell R. Esposito, P. J. Forcino, Colleen Giammanco, Judy Gray, Joyce Harvey, Norman Harvey, Scott Hirsch, John Adam Kanas, Jim Karagiorgis, Regina A. Keller, Stanley Klausner, M.D., Jack Leahy, Michael J. Leckie, Scott M. Lunski, Marge Magner, Ron Malone, Burt Manning, Tom McAteer, Jr., David Neeleman, Thomas Ockers, Christopher J. L. O'Connell, James L. Orsini, Elizabeth R. Plonski, Professor John Quelch, Robert G. Reiss, David Scordato, Philip J. Shapiro, Greg Smith, Gary Steinkohl, Walter Timoshenko, Edward Travaglianti, Raymond S. Troubh, David "Doonie" Waldron, Barry Warren, Samuel N. Wender, Nancy Westbrook, Josh Weston, and Aline Wolff.

INTRODUCTION

Being at the top of your game is more crucial than ever, both for individuals and companies. The business environment is so uncertain that no one can afford to miss a step. Some forces are out of our control—recessions, cutbacks, layoffs. But being the best we can be at our job is not. We have total control over that. Whatever stage you're in with your career—whether you're looking for a promotion, trying to stand out, starting a new business, or recently laid off—this book will help you get on track, get results, and move faster and more efficiently.

I work with CEOs and their teams seven days a week, I hear their challenges and see firsthand what makes them successful. I've found that the Six Fundamentals I identify in the book are useful for anyone working in an organization.

So often in business, I see a disconnect between concept and follow-through. There are lots of ideas, but not enough execution. This is a major focus of my consulting work, and it is one of the primary focuses of *The Six Fundamentals of Success.*

The gap between devising a strategy and implementing it almost always involves middle and senior managers. Sometimes we walk in the door of an organization with the goal of developing strategy. But just as often we come into a company behind a big consulting firm, and find a $10 million plan going nowhere. What happened? We started to recognize a consistent problem—poor discipline around the fundamentals of getting the job done right.

Getting the job done right is critical to a company, and critical to you as an individual. Each of us has a part to play in his or her organization. Organizations that do well pay higher salaries, provide better benefits, and are more fun to work at. People who do the job right get recognized, get promoted, and make more money. It is a tremendous validation of their talent and hard work.

I've gathered together the nearly one hundred rules in the pages of this book over thirty years in business working with managers and leaders. I have organized them under the umbrella of the Six Fundamentals that I've discovered to be at the foundation of all business success.

Living these rules will require discipline. They're easy to understand, but hard to do consistently. When you are learning to do something physical, you do it over and over again, and your muscles start to remember it; it's called muscle memory. Athletes and their coaches leverage this phenomenon. They drill their sport's fundamentals so that in the heat of competition, the athlete's muscles "remember" what to do, while the athlete focuses on execution. Incorporate a similar strategy to remember performance fundamentals. Set up a daily workout of fundamentals. Choose one or two of the rules and focus on them for a month. Then choose one or two more.

Whether you are working for a paper company, in the health care industry, for a retail outlet or a law firm, your days are filled with pressure. Drilling with the fundamentals will make them second nature so you can perform at your best, even when under pressure and surrounded by distractions.

I'd enjoy hearing about your experiences applying the fundamentals. Please e-mail me at fundamentals@stuart levine.com. You can also visit our website at www.stuart levine.com. Thank you.

—Stuart R. Levine

THE SIX
FUNDAMENTALS
OF SUCCESS

Make Sure You Add Value

dding value to an organization means you increase its worth and its capacity to serve its customers. A company's worth is linked to its profit potential. So if you help the organization make more profit than it does now, you're adding value. And if you add value, you'll be more valuable to the company. Practicing the rules in this section—whether it's "Act like an owner," "Complete one important thing every day," or "Stop financial hemorrhaging"—will increase your individual worth as an employee, and, in turn, make the company worth more. And there's nothing your boss likes more than increased corporate worth. It's one of the fundamental ways you can advance your career, and increase your own paycheck. (Note: In the not-for-profit world, this translates into financial stability. Even museums strive for a "profit" margin in order to maintain their treasures and acquire new ones.) You can increase your organization's value in four ways: help it sell more, cut costs, get higher prices, and improve quality for the customer. All of this is a balancing act because if you cut costs indiscriminately, you might be cutting quality so much that you lose customers.

You can add value from any level. In fact, often you're uniquely positioned to do this. A server at a major chain restaurant once suggested a change that eliminated a liaison position between the kitchen and waiters and saved the company almost half a million dollars a year system-wide. She was able to do this because she lived on the front lines every day. The people at the corporate office would never have seen it. This kind of input is vital to a company.

The surest way to add value every day is to make sure at least part of your daily work contributes to a strategy. Business strategy is designed to increase an organization's value, so by working on a strategy for at least part of every day you know you're adding value.

To make adding value part of your daily actions and behavior:

- Know how your organization creates value for the customer and how you fit in.
- Understand how your company spends and makes money.
- Focus on the things that are important to adding value.
- Care passionately about customers.
- Continuously improve your skills so you can keep finding new ways to add value.
- Come up with and test new ideas.

See your customer as a person

In order to care about your work, you've got to see how you add value to the customer. Who is the customer and what does she want? What need does your organization meet? What's your customer's life like? For example, if you do billing for a cardiac health center, your customers are usually over fifty years old. They probably have children who care about them and grandchildren who want them around for a long time. Ask your team to think about people in their families who might fit the profile. How would your sister or dad feel coming into the cardiac health center? How does your work make things better or worse for that person? Start from the moment the customer gets your product or service, work backwards, and chart the pieces that come together to deliver it. Where do you fit? Who relies on your team? What happens if you're late? How does it affect other departments? How does it affect your customer?

If you and your team know how your contribution fits in the process, it'll be easier for you to see how your work is important. People give their best to work that's important. So do you.

Know your industry

Know your industry and your company's position in it.

1) Read the business section of the newspaper, watch the business media, and stay current with economic trends that impact your industry. Don't ignore global trends. They affect your organization as well.

2) Read your industry's trade publications, even if you have to borrow your boss's copy.

3) In talking with clients and suppliers, listen to what they have to say.

Spend a few minutes each morning reviewing the news to grasp the top-line trends. If you see an article that might interest a colleague, highlight the pertinent information and send it to her. Add a note about how it could be useful (especially if you're sending it to your boss or a client). Bringing someone's attention to what's relevant helps others, and shows people around you that you understand the industry. They'll see you in a different and better way.

As you scour the media or talk to people in your industry, you'll develop a fuller grounding in the deeper implications of actions and events. And as your understanding of your industry grows, your broadened perspective will help you make better decisions faster.

Develop your financial IQ

It's crucial to understand the language of money to add value to an organization. It will help you strengthen your performance and confidence and further your career.

1) Identify a financial point person in your organization who can help you to gather and interpret financial information.

2) Make sure you and everyone on your team can read a balance sheet and understand its implications.

3) Ask your boss for the profit margins* of all your organization's products and services. Find out how your team might increase or threaten that margin.

4) Start meetings with a financial update, such as reviewing monthly business results. Explain what the numbers mean and how the people in the room can affect the numbers. When wrapping up, connect the meeting's discussion back to financial performance.

5) Coach team members one on one about how their work affects financial performance. Ask, "Do you understand how your work affects our ability to achieve results?"

6) Don't assume everyone understands financial terms. Whenever you use such terms, define them. When someone else uses an unfamiliar term, ask him or her to explain.

7) Never pretend to understand something you don't. Ask for clarification when you need it. It shows people on your team that it's okay to "not know," and that asking for help is a sign of confidence, not ignorance.

Demand strong "numbers literacy" from yourself and your team. Make yourself an integral part of your organization's financial health.

---

* Net income as a percentage of sales or revenues.

Work with a sense of urgency

There are important things at stake every day—your organization's goals, your department's financial performance, the customer's experience. Work fast, work hard, and do as much as you can do well.

Urgency isn't mania, however—don't crank out work just to cross it off your list. Work hard to produce a high standard of quality. Let your sense of urgency come from a genuine passion for delivering something of value to your customer, your team, or your work. Urgency should be paired with pride in getting it right.

Working this way gives you and the people around you energy. You'll finish the day feeling you've accomplished a lot.

Make yourself promotable

To get promoted, you need to already have developed the skills needed to do the job you are working toward. Voluntarily assume more and more of the responsibility. Learn as much as you can from the people currently working in that position by asking them questions or pitching in to help. Usually, they will be happy to have your interest and assistance. And they can be important allies in helping you make the move when the time is right.

Get your boss's support by helping her achieve her goals. As you pursue your career goals, don't give your boss any reason to think you don't care about doing great work in your current job. You'll need your boss's support to get the job you want and if you're not doing your current job well, there is no way you'll be promoted. So be sure your current work doesn't suffer, and that you make your boss look good. That's your job today.

If possible, train and develop the person who is likely to replace you. If you want to move up, make sure it's clear to decision-makers that you've groomed a replacement. Don't avoid this to make yourself seem indispensable. It doesn't work that way. Training your successor will get you promoted instead.

Create your own performance dashboard

How do you know if you're on track to meet your goals? You need a system to assure that you get there. Think of a car's dashboard. There are gauges and indicators that tell you whether critical functions are working. Do you have enough gas? How hot is the engine? How fast are you traveling? This information "snapshot" is designed to monitor your car's performance and help you make necessary repairs before the car breaks down. Design a dashboard for your job performance as well. Use it to see if you're getting where you want to be this quarter or this year.

Set goals that you'll accomplish *within* a given time period. Goals should always be timed and measurable—you either meet them or you don't within the time you defined. The only exception is "learning goals," such as presentation skills, which can be more difficult to measure. Discuss your goals with your supervisor. Ask for her agreement that the goals you've set line up with how she'll assess your performance. Include any learning goals you've established to emphasize their importance in your professional development. Here are a few examples.

By the end of this quarter:

Increase productivity by 10%

Decrease project budgets by 15%

Strengthen meeting management, presentation, and coaching skills (learning goals)

Get the information you need to make sure you're making progress toward your target. If you're falling behind, step on the gas or reevaluate the route you're taking.

By measuring your accomplishments you not only work better, you can also better communicate your progress to your boss—the person who assesses your salary and bonuses. Never assume your boss knows what you're getting done. Each quarter, share your dashboard results.

Know what's on your boss's dashboard

Helping your boss achieve his goals is good for your career. It's also your job. When designing your performance dashboard, include at least one goal that specifically supports one of your boss's. Even if your boss doesn't keep a formal dashboard, his performance is being measured. When you schedule time to review your personal dashboard, be sure to ask how your department's performance is measured and what your boss needs to achieve.

Here's an example. At a small retail chain, a new CEO was chosen to turn the company's financial performance around. She worked with the senior leadership team to define a number of initiatives. Her long-term survival depended on being able to assess store-by-store progress. The controller saw her challenge and made it his goal to retool the financial reporting system so the CEO could get the information she needed to make better, faster decisions. This move enabled her to take actions that saved the company $50 million that year.

If you have employees who report to you, tell them your goals so they can help you achieve them.

Create a plan

Create a personal plan every year that shows what you need to get done in the next twelve months. Make sure your plan lines up with your dashboard goals and your boss's expectations for your team. Divide the goals into monthly action milestones. If it involves your team, ask for input in setting those milestones.

At the start of each month, create a mini-operating plan that shows what you will have to do to meet your monthly milestones. Prioritize it. Then schedule it. Next, create a detailed "To Do" list for the upcoming week. Integrate this into your monthly calendar or PDA or personal or-ganizer—whatever works for you. (Always do it in the same place.) By Sunday night, create a detailed list for the next week.

Each evening before you leave work, review your list for the day and cross off what you've done. Reschedule what you weren't able to complete, add in new work that's come up, and review the next day's list, and the week's list.

When you start to feel overwhelmed, review what you've accomplished in the previous four weeks. Planning ahead and tracking your progress day by day, and week by week, will help you to get more done and move steadily toward a larger objective.

Do what matters most first

The squeaky wheel gets the grease, as the saying goes. But six e-mails and ten voice mails don't necessarily make a decision or project the most important issue in your in-box. Great managers know how to identify what's truly important and do it first. Take your "To Do" list and rate each item. Keep it simple: use an *I* for important things and a *T* for time-sensitive things (use both if an item is important and time-sensitive). Do things that you rated as both important and time-sensitive first. Do things rated important, but not time-sensitive second. Do things that are rated time-sensitive, but not important, after you've done everything else. Delegate everything you can that is not "important" but still needs to be done.

Important things help companies make money in seven ways:

- Getting new customers
- Keeping existing customers
- Delivering great value
- Improving quality
- Reducing costs without compromising value
- Managing risk
- Advancing the business strategy

Time-sensitive things are more pressing. If you don't take action now, you will lose an opportunity or suffer a negative consequence. For example: You have to put in your request for new office supplies by noon every Friday. On Friday at 11:45, the deadline is pressing but it's only *important* if you're in immediate need of new supplies or equipment.

Good bosses expect you to handle 98 percent of your time management decisions. If it is a high-stakes situation and the priority isn't clear, get your boss's input. Otherwise, use your best judgment.

Prioritizing can help you focus on what matters most. Effective managers not only work hard, but work smart. They do this by making the right choices on where to focus their energy and their time at any given moment.

Complete one important thing every day

How many times do you end the day feeling like you didn't accomplish anything? That feeling you get when you review your "To Do" list and you haven't crossed off anything important on it. You fought fires all day and got nowhere. It's draining.

Do at least one important thing every day. Refuse to leave until it's done. It's okay if it wasn't on your list, as long as it's truly important. If you have the chance to spend time with a major customer or your boss asks your team to support another team that's facing a tough deadline, do it. If it involves your team, send an e-mail thanking them for their hard work. By e-mailing them, you've done something else important—you've given them energy and set them up for success the next day.

You need to motivate yourself before you can motivate a team. Knowing you did something that added value will give you a feeling of accomplishment as you end your workday. Give this to yourself every day.

Prepare

Preparation takes work. Far too many people "wing it"—they make it up as they go along. Slick improvisation can't replace the clear, pointed communication that occurs when you're prepared. Waiting until the last minute and cramming your prep time into fifteen minutes is too much of a risk. This is real life, not your exams. Don't cram.

• Define your goals and those of the other person (or group). If you have questions about the other person's goals, call or e-mail to make sure you know what he or she wants.

- Think through what's at stake. Is the other person paying for your time? Are you working on a business lead that could result in substantial income? Knowing this will help you decide how much time to spend beforehand.

- Do your homework. If you are preparing a presentation, think through your comments. If you are preparing a team meeting, read the materials you receive in advance and make notes. If you are meeting with a prospective client, research the company. Find out how to spell and pronounce the names of the people you're meeting. Know who will be in the room.

- Anticipate questions and plan responses.

- Practice several times, even if the "meeting" is just a one-on-one conversation. Quickly running through what you want to say will help you stay focused and clear.

- Make a list of what you'll need to bring with you and run through it just before you leave.

People can tell when you haven't given the meeting much thought. Prepare and you'll have a better outcome.

Be flexible

Businesses used to prepare five- and ten-year business plans. Now the majority do detailed plans only for the coming one to three years at most. They recognize that events shift too quickly to plan further out than that. Smart companies focus on developing agile teams with the skills to change course if necessary. Responding intelligently to changes in the world around them gives them an edge.

The same is true in your day-to-day work. No matter how much you plan and prioritize, there will be days when the unexpected pulls you off course. That's life. Some events we can't control. Accepting this is a sign of professional maturity.

You need to strike a balance between planning ahead and being flexible. Don't be derailed by unimportant things. Use predetermined goals and priorities to stick to the task at hand. But if something more important emerges, roll with it. If your boss thinks something that has come up is more important than what you are working on, but you don't, let him know. If he still asks you to adjust your priorities, be responsive and give it your all. As long as you're doing work that matters, at the end of the day you will feel like you accomplished something.

When an athlete doesn't stretch before a competition, his risk of injury increases dramatically. If your concept of work is rigid, you, too, are much more likely to get hurt. Stretch your concept of work. As your last "To Do" for each day, include this one: *Whatever it takes*.

Timing is everything

In football, when a running back sees a hole, he runs through it. A star running back is a master of timing. He has to be moving at the right speed and be in the right spot when the hole opens up. Then he accelerates and bursts through the opening. A second early or late and there's no hole. Poor acceleration and he doesn't make it through.

This sense of rhythm and timing is true in business at every level. The trick is to recognize when timing is important. It might mean coming out with a new product before your competitor. Or spotting an opportunity in your company and grasping it. You have to act quickly because in a competitive marketplace, if you don't act, someone else will. The follow-up to any meetings with customers or clients is equally important. If you make a strong first impression, but don't follow up in a timely manner, your advantage is lost. If you don't respond to your boss in a timely manner, he may be annoyed or disgruntled with you, even if your work in the end is excellent. Stay attuned to the timing and rhythm of your business or workplace.

Your boss isn't your mother

When your boss asks you to take responsibility for something, it means she trusts you. Her trust translates into an opportunity to show your value. If you run into a roadblock, try to solve it yourself or with the help of others before running to your boss for help. Ask what result she expects and take ownership of getting it done.

Let me give you an example. Your boss asks you to collect and synthesize data from the team for the monthly activity reports so she can review them the first week of every month. You send out an e-mail to those involved, letting them know you'll need the reports by the first day of every month. On the second day of the month you're still missing three reports. Owning the result means that you follow up with those three people until you get what you need for the report. It's shocking how many managers will go to their boss and say, "I can't give you the data yet because I haven't received all the reports." Your boss didn't ask you to send an e-mail requesting the data, she asked you to get it. Own the result. How? E-mail everyone again before their reports are due. Walk the floor in person the day before to remind them again and to make clear you are serious about the date. Own the project. This is what being a manager, as opposed to a "task doer," is all about.

Act like an owner

Successful entrepreneurs lose sleep over winning. Because the business is their own, they've always got the big picture in mind. Yet few details escape their attention. For one, they're constantly thinking about their customers. They tend to dig deeper into everything instead of thinking, "It's not my job." They build strong teams and take care of their people because they see firsthand the impact their employees have on the customer. They have an unrelenting drive to achieve.

To be successful at your job, think like an entrepreneur.

Let me give you an example. One day, a team at a $750 million unit of a Fortune 100 company was doing a routine review of checks going out. Someone noticed they'd overpaid a vendor by twenty dollars. Most of the team thought it wasn't worth their time to chase down the mistake. But one person went back and checked the vendor files. He found that they'd overpaid that vendor by $100,000 over the previous six months. That person was thinking like an entrepreneur.

Large businesses are composed of small businesses. Run your unit like a small business. Take its success personally. Think and act like an owner.

Know the burn rate of key resources

Think of your department's or your team's resources as a tank of gas. For every mile you drive, you burn fuel. You probably know about how many miles you get per gallon in your car. This is the burn rate. Do you know the burn rate for your key resources at work?

Let's say you have a three-hour staff meeting Monday mornings. If you have a staff of ten and they each make $60,000 a year plus benefits, office space, etc., then your cost for the meeting is about $400 per hour. Factor in that the average employee generally contributes at the rate of

2.5 times what he costs, so the collective *value* of their time is $1,000 per hour. Let's say someone is a half hour late, and everyone has to sit and wait. You just burned $500. Does that person always have trouble getting in on Mondays? If it happens fifty times a year, this habit costs $25,000 annually. Multiply that number by four if you're dealing with senior executives.

List your ten key resources. For example:

Space (office space, production facilities, inventory space)
Technology (printers, software licenses, major production technologies)
People (you, team members, internal suppliers)

Tell your boss that you'd like to know the value of your key resources so you can make the most of them. Work with him or her to get the specific hourly, weekly, or monthly value of each from the finance department (they probably have this figured out already). Then, if you are in charge of a group or department, review the numbers whenever you make decisions about how to achieve your department's goals and think about burn rates. Collectively, they're your tank of gas. It's your job to get as far as possible on that tank of gas. If your boss is in charge of the group or department think about ways you can help him use those resources effectively. In the beginning it will require discipline. Write down the numbers and do the math. But as you practice, it will become second nature, and you'll get more bang—more mileage—for your department's dollar.

Stop financial hemorrhaging

Is your organization losing money or not hitting its margins? Your company, division, or group may be bleeding internally. Learn to spot financial hemorrhages. Cash may be slipping away, and the reason isn't always obvious. If hemorrhages are not clamped, they will keep bleeding cash indefinitely.

A classic example is employee turnover. When an employee resigns, it can cost up to twice his annual salary to replace him. On average, new hires need to stay eighteen months just to cover the cost of their hiring. And these are only direct costs—not taking into account the impact on customer loyalty and productivity. Yet some organizations tolerate a 50 percent annual turnover rate as an acceptable cost of doing business. People aren't staying long enough to pay for their hiring and training, much less make a contribution to profits.

Here are some other ways companies hemorrhage.

• Underutilized resources—space, technology, people, time, and money. If your major asset is a printing press and it's only producing materials 60 percent of the time while print jobs sit waiting for staff signoff, your company's hemorrhaging money. Conduct an audit to make sure you're maximizing your investments.

• Unwillingness to confront overcapacity. Don't drag out the tough choices. If you have too much space, lease it. If you have too many employees, reorganize. Don't jeopardize your entire department, group, division, or firm because of your reluctance to pare staff.

• Client turnover. It costs more to attract a new client than to keep an old one. When sales revenues are the same, but a higher percentage of your sales revenue is coming from new clients, your margin is eroding.

• Cost of rework. When people in your organization have to redo work they've completed it can cause major cost overruns. If you consistently see cost overruns in the same area look for signs of rework, determine what's causing it, and fix the problem.

Analyze the monthly financial reports. If something doesn't seem right, it probably isn't. Partner with a financial person to analyze the numbers. Don't worry that a financial hemorrhage in your area will make you look bad. Everyone has them at times. You look far better showing the business acumen it takes to spot a problem and fix it than letting it persist.

Work smarter

Make doing good work as easy as possible for you and those you work with. It will cut down on frustration because you aren't repeatedly overcoming the same obstacles.

In a large chain restaurant, a bartender complained to his manager that he had to ask the waiters to get coffee for bar customers—during the fast-paced lunch hour everyone wanted coffee and it was holding him up. The manager watched the crew work through the next shift and realized that if he switched the coffee machine with the salad refrigerator in the prep area, the bartender could get his own coffee and the change wouldn't affect the work flow. Bar customers got better service, the bartender got bigger tips, and lunch sales went up at the bar because people got in and out faster.

Start by making a list of the jobs you do often—the ones that will give you the most payback. Then answer this question: what makes this work harder or more time-consuming? Make a list of the barriers to productivity you face. Then think what practical changes would eliminate these barriers. If it's in your power to make the change, make it. If not, estimate the time savings your change will create and the dollar value of the time. Calculate the potential savings and use that information to propose the change to your boss. Encourage your team to think this way too. At your next meeting, take a few minutes to do the exercise I've just described. Tell them they can make any suggestion to simplify or improve their processes as long as it's presented with a sound calculation of how it will save money and how much it will save.

Make your mission possible

Many people look at their company's mission as rhetoric on a poster. These people don't understand a mission statement's power. Their intellectual cynicism is a barrier to leadership. The mission describes your organization's purpose—why everyone comes to work each day. It can be a practical, useful tool.

One management group used it like this. They were evaluating customer survey results when a clear customer preference emerged, one that would cost a lot of money. They rejected the idea because they assumed senior management wouldn't go for it. Then someone pointed out that customer commitment was the centerpiece of the company's mission statement. They reviewed the data and made a practical recommendation that measurably increased customer loyalty without bankrupting the company. This is a mission statement in action.

Know your organization's mission statement. Keep a copy with you in meetings, in your calendar or PDA. Discuss it with your direct reports. Use it to help create ideas or validate the quality of ideas other people bring to the table. When people debate different options, use the mission to take a stand on one of them. Commit to trying this at least once. Answers will come clearer faster. Your mission statement created the blueprint for your business plan so it's only logical that it should help you make solid business decisions.

If your organization doesn't have a mission statement or you feel the one you have is just rhetoric, pull a group together to create a new one. And if management pushes back, don't give up.

Governance starts with you

You're working in a new world today. Every time you provide information that will feed into the way your organization's leaders make decisions, someone is scrutinizing your work as never before. Everyone has been affected by the unethical choices and "aggressive" accounting practices of relatively few business leaders. The fact that it's not your fault doesn't mean it won't affect you. People have lost faith in financial reporting practices and that affects your organization's ability to attract investors, lenders, or donors. As a result, it takes longer to do things and it's harder to compete. It will take a long time to re-build credibility. This process starts with you.

A lot of managers think collecting pieces of perform-ance information like "monthly employee turnover" or "inventory on hand" is a waste of time—busywork to keep the bean counters happy. But investors want to know how your company is doing against key financial meas-ures, and the CEO and CFO must certify that the infor-mation you put out is accurate. In fact, they may be held legally liable if the information is wrong. They can't pos-sibly know firsthand the performance that feeds into every organizational metric. They and the organization's in-vestors must be able to trust the competence and integrity of the people working in the organization.

Beyond the highly visible credibility and legal issues, there's another very practical reason to be cautious with these reports. The CEO and the board can't make good decisions about your organization's future without good information about what's really happening now. The bet-ter the information, the better the decision-making. On all levels, it's in your best interest to take care and make sure performance data coming from your area is sound.

Invite and value feedback

Receiving negative feedback is an important learning opportunity. It's free, usually very specific, and customized to your needs. And yet, it can be hard to come by.

Why is that? Look at the other side of the equation. How do you feel when you offer constructive criticism? Most people dread giving negative feedback, just as many people dread receiving it. The person being addressed may become defensive. As a result, you think, "Well he's not listening anyway. Why bother?" You make a mental note never to candidly approach that person again.

Remember when you're on the receiving end that the other person is uncomfortable too. Show that you recognize his or her situation. When someone offers feedback, say, "Thanks, I appreciate that." He or she will know you're listening. If you disagree, rather than becoming defensive say, "I appreciate your telling me and I promise to think about it." Then do. Often when you get some distance from the conversation, you can see more truth in the comment. In any case, close the conversation by thanking him and telling him he can approach you anytime.

Confident professionals always stay open to well-intended feedback. It strengthens relationships and helps you to grow.

"Replay the tape"

After a game, football coaches review the day's videotape relentlessly. They watch over and over again to see what worked and what did not, who executed properly, and who did not. They use what they learn to design new plays, improve players' skills, and plan the next week's practice.

This technique can be effective in business too. Replay the tape at the end of your day. In your mind, spend a few minutes in the evening thinking through the conversations you had during the day, and the actions you took.

Set aside a specific time to replay your daily "tape." It

could be during your commute home, or after dinner, or before you prepare for bed. Think about how you handled challenging situations—what worked and what you'll do differently next time. Reflect on what you learned about others, and about yourself. Commit to improving. Congratulate yourself on the things you did well. Do it every evening. Make it a habit.

Invest in yourself

Take control of your continuing education and personal growth. Every six months, give yourself specific learning goals, and include these on your performance dashboard. (See page 15, "Create your own performance dashboard.") Then design a plan to achieve each goal. Don't focus only on improving your weak spots; concentrate on your strong areas as well. Your natural talents are tremendous assets. Recognize them and maximize what you do well.

Look at your current job. List the skills you need to do well. Next look at your goals. If you want to move up the career ladder, what new skills are necessary for the job you want? Do you need to be able to make more presentations or do a budget for the first time? List the skills you need to learn.

Write three improvement goals for the next six months—two that will improve performance in your current position, and one that will help you get promoted to your next job. At least one of those goals should focus on one of your strengths.

Next, brainstorm on how to improve those three skills. Get training if it's available. Identify a person who excels in a skill you've targeted and ask for help. If possible, volunteer for a project team that has a top-level performer. Working with exceptional people can help raise you to their level. Figure out ways to stretch your skills inside and outside of work. Commit your plan to paper.

Too often people wait for their boss to tell them what skills they need. This is a stunning abdication of responsibility. Look in the mirror. Take responsibility and invest in yourself. Your knowledge, skills, and experience are your professional assets. They are your passport to advancement. Manage their development with purpose.

Communicate Up and Down, Inside and Out

Communication helps to bring the best thinking into the right conversations at the right time. It reduces fear and uncertainty and breaks down barriers. It strengthens relationships, improves products, and motivates employees.

In today's world, organizations are faced with new communication challenges. As it has gotten easier to send information around, many people mistake sending and receiving information for communication. They use technology to replace, instead of enhance, communication.

They hide behind e-mail and voice mail to avoid difficult conversations that should take place face to face. As the pace of change creates the need for stronger coordination of efforts, organizations are at risk of experiencing a communication breakdown.

Miscommunication can be disastrous. It can sink careers and even companies. Sometimes miscommunication results when people try to rush you. They may say "I get it," even when you know they really don't get it. Avoid falling into this trap and other miscommunication traps by following the communication rules outlined in this section, such as "Establish a rhythm," "Hear what you're saying," or "Excel at giving feedback." These rules can help you to be a better communicator. Bosses notice great communicators. It's a skill prized in any organization, and one that will set you apart. Effective communication requires an investment of thought about the other person—what specific information he needs, the most appropriate medium, and the goal. Communication is two way. Listening and knowing how you're impacting others is all part of true communication. Human interactions on this level can be complicated. They require skill. But they make organizations better.

Establish a rhythm

Football players, symphony musicians, soldiers—any group that needs to work together seamlessly—must be in sync. The quarterback calls out the play, the conductor sets the tempo, the drill sergeant shouts out the cadence. Leaders create synergy with the rhythm of regular communication. And employees keep it going. Daily e-mail updates, weekly team meetings, and biweekly one-on-ones all create a steady beat. That beat provides the structure and urgency team members need to stay in step with each other. It creates energy and momentum, improving productivity.

Despite distractions and competing priorities, don't postpone regularly scheduled meetings. If you cannot be there or write the message yourself, get a stand-in. Make daily or weekly reports a necessity, via e-mail, on paper, or in person. Read and respond to reports promptly, in a predictable time frame. Make it clear that turnaround is a priority. Keep information flowing consistently. Let your bosses, employees, and peers know what you're doing, what you've done, and what you plan to do tomorrow.

Consistent expectations bring consistent results. The manager sets the pace; the team keeps the rhythm. Use frequent communication to improve your company's timing and precision.

If it's important, say it twice

When a doctor in surgery asks a nurse for O-negative blood, the nurse replies, "I have O-negative blood." Not "Okay, here it is." She repeats the request as part of a process that eliminates error. The stakes are too high for a miscommunication.

When the stakes are high in your world, say it at least twice. Follow up on a conversation with a note. Leave a voice mail and/or an e-mail. You're dealing with people who are juggling a lot of balls. Make sure they get the message and ask for a reply to confirm they did. If you haven't heard back from them and you should have, send a reminder. Look people in the eye when you're speaking with them to confirm you're making a connection. Then ask a question to make sure they got your meaning.

Build redundancy into your communication process, especially when there's a lot riding on it.

Listen actively

Listen actively, not passively. Active listening shows respect. It deepens trust and increases the likelihood that the other person will share information in the future. People too often approach a dialogue feeling they must "win." Such assumptions are one of the reasons we develop poor listening habits, and interrupt.

Watch how people *act* when they're talking. Work to understand what they're telling you. Ask questions. Focus completely on the person speaking. Look him in the eye. Observe his attitude and body language—it's all part of what he's saying. Sometimes people say one thing, but communicate something else through their body language. You need to listen actively to get a proper "read."

CEOs often ask consultants, "What are my people saying?" A great CEO asks, "What *questions* are my people asking?" He knows that questioning demonstrates a deeper level of thinking and a desire to understand.

Listen actively in the next conversation you have. When you replay the tape (see page 50, "Replay the tape"), consider how different the exchange felt. It will assure you of a better outcome.

Hear what you're saying

Have you ever wondered how salespeople do the same pitch week after week and make it sound so natural, as if they're saying it for the first time? Their secret? They focus on really hearing their words.

Sometimes people in business go on autopilot. They're running a tape in their mind. They've made the presentation so many times that they click into Speech #10 on shareholder value and they stop paying attention. Have you ever caught yourself in the middle of a sentence and wondered, "What the heck am I saying?" Stop. Take a breath and begin again—listen to your words. Refocus your comments by saying, "I think my bottom-line point is this . . ." and then listen to yourself—you're asking everyone else to. It will keep you focused and help you make a sharper point.

This is especially true when you're presenting to a group. Even if you're reading to the audience, listen to yourself as you speak. You'll sound more natural and sincere.

Read the impact you have on others

How do you affect people around you? When you're speaking do they seem to get tense? Do you see people shut down or start looking at their wristwatches? Do their eyes glaze over? Or are you giving them energy and making them excited? Our words and actions affect other people—sometimes positively and sometimes not. To lead others, you need to know the impact you're having on them. Learn to watch their body language when you speak. If you're not achieving the impact you want in a one-on-one conversation, ask the other person about it:

"You seem to be confused. I'm afraid I'm not getting my point across as well as I should. Can you help me understand what I'm not conveying?" This is a critical question. Ask it genuinely so people know they can be honest with you. Then listen carefully to their answer. Often people will give you information about how your style affects them. If you're affecting one person this way, you are probably doing the same thing to others. Thank the person for their candor. If you stay open to what the other person says to you, these conversations can give you an "ah-ha" moment of understanding that dramatically improves your ability to communicate with others.

Once you have this information, act on it. Tell your boss or a mentor of the feedback that you got. Ask for his or her reaction, and develop a strategy for improving.

Pick your battles

There are always plenty of battles to fight, wherever your opinion doesn't carry the day. But you can't win them all. Moreover, if you're always fighting, you'll alienate people around you who you'll need to help you get business results. You could get wounded in the process. Worse, people will stop listening to you. "It's just Fred, he always finds something to argue about."

Don't try to win every battle. Don't fight for something unless it's truly important to you. Stop and think. Better to let whatever it is go and save your energy for something that truly matters. When you do decide to fight for an idea, you'll find it easier to get support from others because they know you only take on battles that you believe strongly in.

When you do decide an issue is worth fighting over, be careful not to undermine long-standing relationships, or to make an issue personal. To do so is unprofessional, even if a colleague does resort to an individual attack. You are conducting business, not waging war. Avoid a "take no prisoners" approach. Remain polite, and win by the strength of your arguments and support. The best way to win a battle is through preparation, planning, and gathering support before a decision is to be made.

No surprises

How much communication a boss wants varies, but no boss likes surprises. If something happens that concerns your boss, don't let him hear about it from someone else. Here are a few things you should tell your boss right away:

- A key person announces he's leaving to join a competitor's operation.
- It looks like you're not going to hit your quarterly numbers (show him before he shows you).
- There's been a misstep in a key client relationship.

- You're about to contact one of your boss's contacts for a favor.
- A key mistake has been made by you or your team. (See page 136, "Learn from your mistakes.")

Your boss trusts you to make sure he has the information he needs when he needs it. When that trust gets violated, it damages his faith in you and your working relationship. Always be the one to deliver the news, and let your team know that you expect the same from them.

Say thank you

Sometimes good business behavior is the result of good parenting. When we were young, our parents taught us to say thank you because they wanted us to have a productive, happy life.

When someone does something special for you, send him a handwritten thank-you note. It may take a few minutes, but the impact will be lasting. Keep a supply of thank-you notes in your briefcase or desk with postage stamps. Sit down and write the note as soon as the impulse occurs. People will remember.

If someone helps you prepare for a job interview, send an immediate thank-you note, and follow up later with a phone call or note advising him how things turned out. People invested in your long-term goals appreciate knowing the final outcome.

Don't make insincere gestures. They erode your credibility. Send thank-you notes when they're genuinely appropriate.

Respond to calls and e-mails within twenty-four hours

Commit to returning calls and e-mails within twenty-four hours. Make it a personal standard and hold yourself accountable. Start by changing your voice mail message to indicate that you will reply within this time frame. This simple step instantly creates accountability.

Then make it happen. Whenever you listen to a message, make a note in your phone log. There are many organizer style options. Use whichever one works for you, but keep the information in the same place. Whenever you check your voice mail, make sure you're writing down the day and time of the call, the person calling, the message, if and when you returned it, and if you delegated the response to someone else. Review this list and your e-mail in-box at least once a day to make sure you've responded to each message that requires a response. If you're waiting for input from someone else, reply to let the person know you're waiting for information and give her a sense of when she'll hear from you.

If you don't need to speak with the person, send an e-mail reply or leave a voice mail after business hours with the necessary information. If it's something you can delegate, leave a message about the handoff. "Tom Allen, my assistant, will get back to you. If you haven't heard from Tom by the end of the week let me know."

Commit to meeting this goal unless you're going to be out of the office. In that case, change your voice mail and e-mail to let people know who to call in your office while you're gone. Responding promptly tells people you can manage your time, and you respect theirs.

Write an elevator speech

Be able to say why your company or division stands out in the time it takes to ride from the first floor to the tenth on an elevator. Then tell the story whenever you get a chance. It's good for business, and for winning clients or customers, and it will make your next recruiting push easier too.

All organizations have a value proposition—a unique combination of attributes that makes them stand out. Is yours documented? If not, go to your organization's website and then visit competitors' sites. Make notes about what makes your organization different. Has your company won any service awards? Do you have a unique proven approach? More experience or flexibility? A fuller range of services? Write down who your customer is, what you give them, and why they should choose yours over another organization.

Now convert it to plain talk. Think of a story that shows the value proposition in action. Here's an example from an HMO:

> I work at Morningsun Health, an HMO that specializes in strong service. Let me give you an example. A new member called a month ago and we found out she'd just paid for a wheelchair so we called the supplier to get it covered retroactively. She had only called to find out if her drugs would be covered.

This story happens to be true. Good organizations have good stories. Figure out how to tell yours.

Note: If your organization has no formal value proposition statement, start a process to define one. At a minimum, share your elevator speech with others on your team and make sure they understand the power of a consistent public message.

Share the good news—and the bad

The CEO of one small business had a talented team around him that he'd built through several years of strong growth. He regularly told them any good news about the company's performance and future prospects. Then there was an economic downturn and growth slowed. The CEO met one on one with each key person on his staff. He explained the economy's impact, outlined his plan of action, and asked them to contribute their thinking. Earnings diminished for a time. But he didn't lose a single employee.

In fact, team members upped their individual efforts to help the company move forward.

Some managers only communicate what is going well. They're like cheerleaders who create an atmosphere that's optimistic and energetic, if slightly unrealistic. Other managers only communicate what is going poorly, creating an atmosphere that's solution oriented, but negative. Both types of communication are vital. Sharing successes keeps people motivated. Sharing challenges provides an opportunity for everyone to participate in the solution. Well-rounded communication results in a confident and focused environment. Don't limit yourself by conveying only one kind of news.

Admitting things aren't going well can make you feel vulnerable, and it requires courage. But telling the truth, especially when it's difficult, builds trust.

Cut to the chase

Consider this:

Business briefings are usually one page long.
CEOs schedule their time in fifteen-minute increments.
In the last twenty years the typical sound bite has gone
   from forty-three seconds to nine.

You must be brief to be heard.
It takes time to think clearly and sequence your ideas.
That's why most people don't do it. When you don't,

you're asking the audience to synthesize the ideas and data so you don't have to. It can anger them. The danger is that they'll stop reading or listening.

Do a short outline to prepare for important conversations, memos, reports, and even e-mails. Make it a habit. Define your message, the ideas and facts that are important to understanding it, and the sequence that best delivers it. If there's a lot of information, cut it into sections and title each section to help the reader see the sequence of ideas. If you're preparing a conversation, use these titles to structure your agenda. If you're asking for something, make the question clear. Making the other person guess means you won't get what you're looking for the majority of the time.

The higher up in an organization your audience, the more critical it is that you know what you want to say, say it crisply, and ask for what you want.

Ask your colleagues and team
what they think

Sometimes in day-to-day work, it may feel like you don't
have the time to get input from people around you. But
take the time to bring their intelligence into the process—
it always pays off. If you've done your job and given them
the big picture all along, their input will show you things
you might miss. They can spot barriers to implementation. They can see opportunities to leverage existing relationships.

Here are some of the times when to make sure you ask
for their input:

- Setting a new policy
- Identifying new customers to pursue
- Improving an existing process
- Evaluating a new technology
- Determining skill needs and training opportunities
- Assessing potential resource cuts in your area

Those you work with have a different and critical perspective. Ask for it.

Stay open to other viewpoints

When someone sees things differently than you do, allow for the possibility the other person may be right. Staying open to other possibilities can save you from the humiliation of having been adamant when it turns out you were wrong. It also fosters the respectful exchange of ideas.

When you disagree with someone, it's important to let him know how you feel. It's also important to say it in a way that stays open to his views. Tell him, "I have a different take." You stop short of saying, "I disagree," which implies you think the other person's wrong. "I have a different take" says, "You might be right, but let me tell you what I see." By doing so, you remain open to his point of view. If he still sees things differently, you might go one step further, explaining why your point of view makes more sense. Use facts to support your position and be specific. If you still disagree, the person with the most authority should make the decision. If it's you, temper the fact that you're overriding the other person by admitting that there's no clear right or wrong, but since you're responsible for the decision you need to use your best judgment. It's always good to ask him to support your decision as well. If the reverse is true, back down gracefully, and offer to support him.

It's healthy to challenge ideas. A constructive debate often yields the best business decisions. People are doing their best to make sound judgments in an environment where we rarely have all the key information. It's possible to disagree and still respect another viewpoint.

Excel at giving feedback

There's no better way to get what you want than to ask for it. Feedback is a great way to tell your colleagues and your team what you're looking for. But it has to be delivered well.

Try these techniques.

• Let those you work with know you like to give feedback often so they'll know how they're doing.

• Ask permission to give feedback and let the other

person set the time. Both these steps give the other person power and make it easier for him to stay open.

• Even if the feedback is negative, begin with the positive: "You've learned a lot in the past few months and I can see you're committed to doing good work." It's easier to hear negative feedback if you pair it with the positive. It's also valuable to give positive feedback all by itself—telling someone what he's doing right is a great way of reinforcing good performance.

• Give feedback with supporting data, whenever possible. For example, "Your customer satisfaction rating is 65 percent and the average is 75 percent. I'd like to give you some ideas on how to bring your rating into line with the average." Hard facts help to depersonalize feedback.

• Be fast and to the point. If your feedback drags on, it'll start to feel like a flogging.

• Be specific. Don't say, "Nice job running the meeting." Instead say, "In the meeting, when you told Kelly you'd handle her concern one on one, that was a terrific way of keeping things on track."

• Focus on what people do instead of speculating about what motivates them. How they behave is what's relevant. They'll be justifiably defensive if you judge them on a more subjective level.

• Give negative feedback in private and positive feedback in public.

• Invite feedback from your direct reports and show

them how to take it constructively. When someone approaches you with a comment, stay open, listen, thank her, and invite her to give feedback again. (See page 48, "Invite and value feedback.") If it's a valid comment, work to make a change. Nothing empowers people more than feeling they can tell you what they think and then seeing it have an effect.

Face up to difficult conversations

Difficult conversations are a part of life. If faced with one, don't hide behind someone else. Take responsibility. Giving a colleague sensitive feedback, letting someone know that he won't get a promotion, dealing with a belligerent employee or customer—these are complicated, uncomfortable, excruciatingly human interactions in business. They're also completely necessary.

Take the example of two entrepreneurs who started a business together. They made many mistakes on their first project. To get the project back on track, they had to have a series of tricky conversations with employees, customers, and others. One of them handled these "talks." The other avoided them. The first man built a reputation with vendors and employees as a straight shooter. The other was perceived as weak and secondary to the first.

Handle these situations directly with honesty and compassion. It's normal to be uncomfortable. Prepare notes about what you're going to say. Think through potential reactions and possible responses. Always have such conversations privately, discreetly, and in person. There's no need to flog people publicly. They will accept feedback more readily when they don't feel attacked. Stick to your agenda; be concise and focus on the specific issue at hand.

Candor counts

Candor is rare. Like most things, its scarcity makes it more valuable. Be honest without being hurtful. It increases your value.

Take Jesse's experience. One day after a briefing, Jesse told a colleague what a great presentation she'd made. Before he knew it, she was checking her ideas with him before presentations. One day Jesse went into her office after a presentation and gave her a piece of negative feedback. She grilled him about exactly what he meant. She seemed irritated, but thanked him in the end. Jesse was a little uncomfortable, but found she started to count on him more, running all types of issues by him because she knew she'd get the truth. As her career advanced, she was helpful to Jesse in his.

When colleagues or team members ask your opinion, give it with sincere respect·and in private. They may not always want to hear what you say, but they'll always come back to you when they need the truth. Develop a reputation as someone "who will give you an honest answer."

Hostile business environments require more communication, not less

If you're walking in a city you don't know very well and find yourself on a totally deserted street, what happens to your anxiety level? It goes up, doesn't it? Our greatest fear in an uncertain environment is isolation; it makes us feel vulnerable to attack. In business there are many uncertain situations—a new boss coming in, the threat of a takeover, an economic downturn, an internal reorganization. The odds are good that you will have to manage a team through at least one of these periods.

When you run into rough or uncertain water, step up

the pace of communication. Without proper information, people draw their own conclusions, and their fictional scenario may be far worse than real life. Paranoia runs rampant if you don't counter it with facts. To complicate matters, people don't listen well when they're afraid. If you don't know what's happening, be honest. If you know, but can't say, don't lie. Simply touch base with those who report to you as often as possible so they don't feel isolated. Remember that what's obvious to you may not be obvious to everyone. Keep in touch with them about what's happening.

Frequent communication creates confidence. It lets people continue to be productive. In an uncertain environment, that's the best protection one can offer.

Express anger constructively

Anger is a legitimate response to some situations. It's important to acknowledge it. But expressing anger and losing control are two different things. Losing control is inappropriate and self-indulgent. It temporarily makes you feel strong, but in the eyes of others it weakens you. It harms relationships, sometimes irreparably. It pushes people away. It causes embarrassment. It compromises your reputation. If you feel yourself losing control, give yourself time to regain perspective by waiting an hour or a day to address the issue.

People never respond well to intimidation. Stay focused on expressing your frustration in a way that promotes better performance from the people you work with. Isolate the core issue and open a dialogue. "I'm angry because it appears you made a decision that cost us a good client. Help me understand what drove your decision." The conversation may give you new insight. If it still seems they were simply out of line, let them know in clear terms. Clarify the facts objectively, respond honestly, and state explicitly how you would like things handled next time. "I disagree with your logic. The action you took lost us a client. In the future, please get input from me or others on the team before making this kind of decision."

An angry outburst makes people defensive. Constructively expressing your concerns lets others stay open to learning and improving.

Resist taking your "emotional temperature" every five minutes

When people feel under the weather, they often take their temperature. It's a good reality check now and then to listen to your body. Such measurement confirms you're reading the situation accurately. But if you're constantly taking your temperature, it's a signal that you may be overreacting to the symptoms or living in fear.

The office is a competitive environment focused on getting results. It's a place for self-sufficiency—not the place for taking your "emotional temperature" every five minutes.

Don't check in with your boss throughout the day looking for approval. Don't copy your boss on every e-mail you send. Don't ask your boss to think through everything on your "To Do" list with you—you're trying to cover yourself by making your boss accountable for your job. Here's the rub: your boss wants *you* to be accountable. You're paid to use your good judgment, communicate appropriately, and get the job done.

Work independently. Stick to a carefully thought-out process to give you confidence in the outcome of each task. If you make a mistake, learn from it—the sun will rise tomorrow. Share key decisions with your boss throughout the process in short e-mails that highlight the information she needs.

If you're managing a high-stakes project and you need input, talk with your boss. Sometimes taking your temperature is smart. But avoid professional hypochondria.

Know How to Deliver Results

Getting results is about knowing what you need to achieve and doing it in the most effective possible way. You do this by following a process—a series of steps that will define how you are going to achieve success. "Don't throw spaghetti against the wall" shows the importance of planning. "Keep meetings focused" reminds you that time wasted in meetings costs money. "Learn from your mistakes" stresses the importance of coming up with a new process if the current one isn't working. Together, the lessons in this chapter will help you to hammer out, and stick to, the best and most efficient way to get things done. If you do this, you'll be viewed as organized and effective, not haphazard and flying blind. And, of course, how you're viewed determines how far you'll go in your company.

You can create a specific process for any project. It will save time, support better decision-making, and let you focus on the creative substance of your work. Following this process should make life easier. If it doesn't, the process needs to be fixed.

Here's an example. A company had been acquired a year ago and a group of managers were on the front line of the integration of the two companies—they were in meetings eight hours a day. During a meeting management training session, they talked about how hard it was to get agendas out in advance of the meeting or meeting notes out within twenty-four hours of the conclusion of the meeting. All of this was part of their process. Finally the trainer asked, "What would it be like now without the process?" Almost in unison, the group replied, "Chaos" and started to laugh.

That's how you can tell a process is working—when people think it's worth the effort. Work on your processes—the ways you go about doing things—until they're useful. Start by identifying the important information that will help you understand what's happening now;

set goals or targets, and decide how to measure your success in achieving them. Include all the key people involved. Once you have established a process, use it in a disciplined way, and work to improve it.

Don't throw spaghetti against the wall

Decades ago a lot of moms used to throw spaghetti against the wall—if it stuck to the wall, it was done. Of course, you lose a lot of spaghetti that way. It's a costly approach that businesses can't afford. Get disciplined about using planning. It takes the guesswork out of getting it right.

Create a planning worksheet when you start a new project. Write the following categories down the left side of a page and leave space to make notes next to them: Objective, Measuring Success, Inclusion, Relevant Facts, Communication, and The Plan. For larger projects, seek access to project planning software. If you can't get it, stick with the worksheet.

Objective: Write a focused description of the objective. Run it by your boss to make sure you understand the assignment.

Measuring Success: Make notes about how you will know you achieved the objective. Be concrete about time, budget, and quality. Check this with your boss.

Inclusion: Write the names of people who'll have a role in making the project work. They become your project team. Also involve people who will be affected by the outcome to make sure they're comfortable with the plan. This gets the best results and eliminates barriers when it's time do the work.

Relevant Facts: List the information you'll need to make good decisions. Get input on this from your team. Consider facts regarding current performance and industry standards or trends. Facts help depersonalize business discussions and make you more confident. That confidence promotes smart risk-taking and innovation.

Communication: An ounce of communication is a worth a pound of rework (having to redo a task or project). Make notes on when and how you will communicate with key people to make sure you're on track. Include your boss on this list.

The Plan: Schedule a planning meeting. Review the objectives and the relevant facts with your team, and decide how to get the job done. Break the approach into steps, assign the work, and set deadlines. Write this information on your worksheet.

This process will improve your results and make life easier. Don't complicate this exercise; using the worksheet should take about ten minutes for small projects. Your ten-minute investment will most likely save days of needless rework.

Data is not knowledge

Thanks to computers, audit trails, accountants, and laser printers, people can dump tons of information or data on you at the push of a button. Probably no more than 10 percent of it is useful.

The word "data" implies that it's been collected in a disciplined way. But even with that discipline in place, initially data is raw. It's the distillation process that's important. You can add tremendous value by synthesizing raw data into the refined information that can improve a company's knowledge.

Before sharing data, set a few minutes aside to think about what the reader needs. Ask yourself a few questions:

- How will the person use it? What's relevant?
- What's new about what I'm forwarding?
- How much does the person I'm sending it to really need to see?
- What's the best way to format or highlight it so its significance is clear?

Send only the new and relevant facts presented in a way that makes them easy to read. Include a short explanation of why you chose to send this information and what additional data is available if the reader wants to see more. When requesting information or data from your team members, ask them to do the same for you.

Accountability begins at the beginning

Provide clear expectations when you make an assignment to team members. You can't hold people accountable after the fact; you have to lay the groundwork from the beginning. Tell people what you want them to do, when you need it done, and how you will measure success. Tell them what the consequences will be if they don't deliver. Be clear about this—if their bonus is tied to good performance, tell them so. Ask them to confirm their commitment in an e-mail so that you both can be sure you are "on the same page."

Ask team members what skills and resources they think they'll need to deliver high-quality work on time and on budget. Resources may include tools, technology, space, time, and people. They should also determine how much input they'll need from you. You're a resource too. (Remember, it's their responsibility to let you know if any of their needs change during the course of the project.)

You are responsible for providing clear expectations, confirming their understanding, getting them what they need, and being available to them. Only then can you hold your team members accountable if the project ends up being late or over budget. If that happens, follow through with the consequences you laid out in the beginning. Without consequences, there is no accountability.

Don't be afraid to be realistic

Have you ever been asked to take on a project that you knew wasn't feasible? In the crushing pace of business, sometimes ideas get passed on for execution before they're fully developed. You can't always keep it from happening, but you can dramatically decrease the number of times you end up stuck with executing impractical strategies. Here's how.

When you receive an assignment, ask your boss what the larger goals are and how success will be measured. Then bring together the people who will be involved in making the project work. Give them all the information you have. Together, determine how you'll carry out the strategy: the specific tasks; the milestones; start and finish dates; and the required people, technology, space, and money. Assign tasks to specific people to make sure the skills you'll need will be available when you need them.

Be creative. Be aggressive. But if the project is really not possible within the constraints you've been given, be honest. Go back to your boss with a realistic plan that achieves her goals. Walk her through the plan and show her specifics. Details keep this conversation from becoming theoretical. This approach will help keep your career on track and will help keep the organization from wasting resources on doomed ideas. If your boss insists that you try to deliver within the original constraints, then try your hardest.

Let your people perform

People tend to push themselves harder than they'll let themselves be pushed by others. This is human nature. Give your team the information they need to determine how they'll contribute. Then let them do it.

Tell the team how your unit will be measured and what they've been asked to do. Set group goals and draw up an action plan. Ask individual team members to set their own goals and write their own action plans. Have them link their strategy to the team's strategy. Make sure everyone sets deadlines and clear measurements for success. Work with each team member in setting up this process. Then stand back and let them perform, without micromanaging them, or stifling their initiative.

This approach pays off in two ways: increased motivation and the development of better planning skills throughout the team. It also lays the groundwork for you to celebrate your team's achievements as they happen.

Establish an agenda

It is remarkable how many meetings take place without an agenda. A well-thought-out agenda is an essential tool that lets participants know what's expected of them before, during, and after a meeting.

When calling a meeting, draft a clear agenda. Include:

- The start and end times
- The meeting purpose
- The participants
- The location (address, room, and floor)

- The order of items to be addressed
- Decisions to be made
- What's expected of participants (who's reporting on what)
- Name and contact information of person hosting the meeting

Always include this information, even for small informal meetings. It sends the message that the meeting will be professional and focused, and that the same professionalism is expected of everyone attending.

Distribute the agenda at least twenty-four hours beforehand so people can prepare—more if the meeting is formal or strategic. This will give everyone time to gather the information they'll need for the discussion. Making expectations clear and giving people time to meet them increases everyone's accountability, as well as their ability to contribute.

Note: If you need to call an impromptu meeting and can't draft an agenda, use the first few minutes to define the group's purpose and agenda.

Keep meetings focused

Learn how to manage meetings. Begin and end on time. Never start a meeting late. One Fortune 50 financial institution locked the doors when meetings were scheduled to begin. Within a week, all meetings were starting on time with every participant in the room. Always leave sufficient wrap-up time at the end of the meeting to make sure you close the meeting on schedule. When reconvening after breaks, begin when you say you will.

Ideas and issues unrelated to your purpose are bound to emerge during meetings. Don't discourage this creative thinking; instead, capture it and save it for later. Write these ideas on a board or easel so that everyone can see them, and give this spot a name, such as the "safety deposit box," or the "idea board." Distribute the safety deposit box contents with the meeting minutes so everyone can think about those ideas later.

Never let anyone hijack the meeting's agenda. If this seems to be happening, restate the meeting purpose and your commitment to end promptly out of respect for the group's time. If someone is still taking you off track, call a break and let him know privately that he's disrupting the agenda, and recommend that he reconvene the group at another time to achieve his objectives.

During the wrap-up phase, summarize agreements and assignments. Ask participants to define what needs to happen next. Make sure that each person knows what she has committed to do, and the deadline she's committed to. Begin your next meeting with a review of all assignments, progress, and accomplishments.

Meetings are expensive. To conduct meetings without achieving their goal is an unnecessary waste. Stay focused.

Infuse meetings with energy

Be positive in meetings. It creates energy and produces momentum. Here's how:

• Recognize your colleagues' achievements and offer your congratulations.

• When the group is asked for suggestions, contribute your best thinking. Listen to others' ideas just as attentively.

• Look whoever's speaking in the eye. Make it clear you are engaged in the conversation or discussion.

- If you like someone's idea, say so. If it's not appropriate in the meeting, take a minute on a break or after the meeting to tell them.
- Address concerns constructively ("Help me understand your thinking" or "Can you share any data that supports your suggestion?").
- Look for solutions. Never shoot down an idea without trying to understand it first.

This kind of dialogue engages participants and builds commitment to a common goal.

Leaders treasure people who bring positive energy to meetings. They increase the team's productivity and follow-through. Never underestimate the impact of a positive attitude—on the team and on your career.

Go for the buy-in

The CEO of a global corporation sat in a room one evening with his ad agency's president to develop a slick, appealing new mission statement that would energize his organization. Then he traveled the world giving out crisp $100 bills to any employee who could recite it. After a year, everyone knew it, but no one was using it. The next year he had key people from within the organization work with him to create another new mission. While developing it, they reached out to people throughout the company to get their input. A year later, the entire organization not only knew the mission, but they were living it—it had become an energizing focal point. And it showed: employee satisfaction went way up, turnover went way down, and new business increased substantially.

Buy-in matters. If you tell people what to do without giving them a say, the outcome suffers. They'll do the work, but not as well. Plus you lose the value of their input. A wider range of thinking and perspective yields a better result.

Getting buy-in begins and ends with seeking input from the right people. Figure out who your key constituents are—the field implementation team, the sales force, your own team—anyone with a major responsibility in its success. Pinpoint the key influencers—the most respected people in those areas. Meet with each one, one on one, to describe what you're trying to accomplish and then ask for his input. (Note: Be sincere. If people sense this is a charade they won't respond.) If you've chosen the right people, their feedback will be beneficial. Use their ideas to improve the plan. If they all disagree with your approach, reevaluate it (they're the most respected for a reason). If they believe in your approach, they'll become internal champions for you.

Trust their input. You'll get the best plan as a result.

Overcome the kings and queens of chaos

Some people in any organization try to prevent change at work by creating chaos—in one company they dub them the kings and queens of chaos. Companies are always evolving. They find better ways to give more value to their customers, and that requires change. But many people resist change because they're afraid of what they don't know. Creating chaos is usually their first response. The chaos kings and queens build a resistance bonfire with "it can't be done," "we've always done it this way," or "let me play the devil's advocate." They will have a thousand reasons not to do something. They breed unfounded fear that new initiatives will fail and harm the organization. Here's how to handle them:

- The kings and queens of chaos get their power from misinformation. Take the power away from these people with frequent communication.
- Give them a voice, but don't let them dominate the conversation.
- Use facts and statistical information to counter baseless claims; this will take away emotion and ease fear.
- Keep everyone who's affected by the new initiative in the loop so they don't start to believe rumors.
- Build accountability—extreme naysayers will let things slip on purpose to prove the initiative was flawed and they were right all along. Make sure they're held responsible.
- Share a positive vision for the future.

These aren't necessarily bad people. They're just afraid. Remove the fear, challenge them, and show them how they can benefit. Most will rise to the occasion and feel more confident for having done it.

Deliver on promises

Deliver on your promises. There are two challenges involved: keeping track of what you've said, and making time in a day packed with other responsibilities. Here are some ideas for both.

KEEPING TRACK

- When you promise to send something, write it down on the back of the person's business card. (If they don't have a card, make a note in your PDA or on one of your own cards—just don't give that card to someone else.)

- Keep a commitment list on your PDA or calendar, separate from other notes. Always bring this to meetings with you.

- Store handwritten notations in the same place.

MAKING TIME

Go in to work fifteen minutes early or stay fifteen minutes late to do your follow-up. If there is a door to your workspace, close it. Forward your phone to voice mail. Don't let anything interrupt you. It takes discipline, but it's worth it. If it's quick, do the follow-up. If it's a bigger commitment, use the time to organize your approach and schedule time to get it done.

A lot of credibility is lost in the gap between what you say and what you do. People may not call you on forgotten promises, but they remember. Follow through.

Behavior speaks for itself

People reveal who they are to you in the first few minutes. Don't ignore what you see—it will come back to haunt you.

One bank manager learned this lesson the hard way. He was recruiting an assistant manager—one of his assistant managers had left the bank without notice for personal reasons and everyone, including him, was stretched to the limit covering the gap. He found someone who seemed to have the right skills. He was desperate to get someone in there, so in his mind, the candidate was already hired. He set up an appointment and asked one of the other assistant managers to join him. The woman was twenty minutes late, but explained that traffic had been bad. He offered her bottled water from the staff kitchen. She took one and put one in her purse, joking that it would be a long trip home. It seemed odd, but it was hot outside. They talked for about twenty minutes during which she interrupted him countless times. In his mind, he excused her behavior, assuming she was nervous. After wrapping up the meeting, he turned to the assistant manager and asked for his recommendation. The assistant manager was dumbfounded. The candidate had been late, openly rude, and had taken something from the office. The manager seemed to be willing to ignore all this because he wanted to get the job filled. The assistant saw it as evidence of how she would perform in the job. In the end, he convinced the manager not to hire her.

Treat people's actions as indicators. While you shouldn't jump to conclusions, don't ignore their behavior either. It's not judgmental to read the signs; it's just smart.

The budget is your friend

The budget and monthly financial reports are invaluable tools. Too many people are afraid of the budget because they know their performance will be measured it against down the road. Remember: it's better to budget and miss than to fly blind. It's the only way you can learn from the result, and improve.

Start by confirming with your boss that your budget goals are in line with the company's. Next, figure out what you need to do to achieve them. Consider all the resources you'll need—space, technology, cash, people. Gather all of your costs and include them in your budget. Validate your assumptions—and any numbers—with your boss. Be clear about when you expect to spend or bring in money.

Here's an example from one company.

Goal: Hire twenty people over the next twelve months, five in each quarter.

Assumptions: On average each hire requires:

- $10,000 for a search firm fee
- Four interviews totaling $400 each (this is based on four hours of your staff's time at $100 per hour)
- One external background check at $500
- One orientation at $300
- $2,500 worth of training during their first month

Your total budget based on these calculations is $13,700 per hire. If the number of hires goes up or down, you can easily calculate how it will affect cost because you've done detailed estimates.

The organization trusts you with its resources. Base the numbers on past experience and research. Never set an unreachable number because you think it will make your boss happy—it sets everyone up for failure. You add more value if you give those around and above you realistic targets. Answer the questions "How much?" and "How many?" as often as possible. Quantify everything that's quantifiable, agree on everything you quantify with your boss, and get it in writing.

Master the financial reports

Most business managers get a monthly package of financial performance information. People use it in different ways. Financial information is crucial because it enables you to monitor how the company—and your division or group—is doing. Make sure you know what's in your financial report, how it's assembled, how your area appears in it, and how your actions affect the numbers. If you are uncertain what the report means, find out. Schedule time with your financial point person or the person who compiles the report to go over it with you. If you don't understand something, say so. Keep asking until you understand. Tell him that you're committed to using the data to get better results, and he'll be happy to invest the time in you.

Regularly review your financial performance with your boss and those reporting to you. If you see performance slipping in an area, analyze why and take action. If there's an overall performance problem, but the cause is unclear, look for a financial hemorrhage. (See page 39, "Stop financial hemorrhaging.") As you analyze the report, ask yourself, "Is there any other information that would help me?"

Ask the finance people for what you need to manage your business better. The finance people want to help you. They succeed when you succeed.

Treat your company's money as your own

Every penny your company spends comes out of the same pot as your bonuses, pay raises, and base salary. Don't spend money on things that won't bring money back into the organization.

• When you travel, don't stay at the most expensive hotel in town and don't order the lobster. Some companies treat this as a perk. But unless your company explicitly tells you so, travel as if you could be spending your pay raise. (You may also find you live healthier if you don't eat big, expensive meals—you might not have to lose a couple of pounds after each trip.)

• At night, turn off your lights, your computer, and anything else that's wasting electricity and money.

• Don't requisition more technology than you need. Let go of the "he who has the most toys wins" mindset. Technological bells and whistles can be seductive, but you don't need a state-of-the-art laptop to run Microsoft Office.

• Can you send that pack out two-day air rather than overnight? Would you request overnight service if you had to pay for it yourself? If the answer is no, use a cheaper service.

These things seem small, but across the organization they're powerful. Consider this. If your company's profit margin is 10 percent and over the course of a year your group saves $10,000 in expenses, that has the same impact on profits as if you generated $100,000 in new sales. Be relentless in eliminating waste.

Manage the risks you take effectively

Heading up a new project can be a great way to get recognized within your company and move ahead. Top management always watches new initiatives closely. But new projects have an element of risk. By definition, there are a lot of unknowns. Learn to manage such risk-taking well. It's a significant career builder.

Here are some effective ways to limit your organization's risk on a new project.

- Make sure you're clear about what reward your organization expects to gain from taking this risk, and when. Ask your boss how much risk is acceptable. How much money can the organization afford to "bet" on the new initiative until you'll cut your losses and pull back? Share this with your team.

* Work to identify as many possible scenarios as you can, especially the most costly or damaging ones. What could go wrong? What opportunities might emerge that you'll need to respond to quickly? What's the likelihood these things will happen? Try to figure out what you don't know. Ask yourself, what if, what if, what if.

* Test your plan. Encourage people to challenge the assumptions on which you based your thinking. Inviting people to poke holes in your plan will help you to make it airtight.

* Make sure everyone understands what you're doing and why—communication is key.

Studies indicate that 46 percent of management and 36 percent of board members don't understand the financial or operational risk related to new investments. Managing risk-taking well creates a competitive edge for you and your organization.

Learn from your mistakes

Imagine you have submitted a report to senior management. Someone catches a substantial error in your team's projections. Who takes responsibility? Does someone immediately assign blame? There is an art to handling mistakes, whether they are made by you personally, or by the team of people who work under you.

First, control the damage.

1) Own the mistake if it is yours.

2) Let your superior know—never let your boss hear it

from someone else. Assess the damage and offer some options for a solution.

3) Immediately notify those affected. Apologize and tell them you will work to ensure that it does not happen again.

How do you keep it from happening again? Answer these questions.

1) Does the mistake represent an individual breakdown or a system breakdown?

2) Is it likely to happen again?

3) Can you improve the process to make sure it won't happen again?

4) What training or communication would help to correct such mistakes in the future?

Last, follow through. Let everyone you work with know what happened, and what changes will be made to make sure it doesn't happen again. It's important not to embarrass anyone here if someone under you was responsible for the mistake. But discussing the problem can help people to learn, eliminate fear, and short-circuit the rumor mill.

When you handle mistakes well, everyone learns, your business processes improve, and your credibility is strengthened.

The power of nice

One senior executive calls "the niceness factor" the single most important factor in his firm's success. It helps to cement relationships inside and outside the company.

Being nice doesn't mean you're weak or unable to get results. It doesn't mean you can't make tough decisions. It does mean you smile at people and say hi when you pass them in the hall. You're fair when things go wrong. You laugh at others' jokes when they are funny. You ask how a colleague's family is doing when you're in the elevator. You wish people a good night when you leave. You should be just as nice to colleagues as you are with customers.

It can help to build up a reservoir of goodwill that could serve you well one day. And it makes work a more pleasant experience. Being nice to others will help draw people to you. They want to associate with you because they like the experience. Being nice is a dramatically underrated technique for improving your effectiveness in your job.

Conduct Yourself and Your Business with Integrity

We all know what The Ritz-Carlton and Starbucks stand for because they invest heavily in building their brand—not just in advertising, but by delivering a consistent experience to the customer. Nothing strengthens a brand more effectively than acting consistently and with integrity. If you act with integrity at some times, and not at others, your brand becomes meaningless.

Your name is your brand in the marketplace. You trade on it every day. A trusted brand gives you the credibility to get things done for your organization. It is not something you can negotiate or barter with. It's absolutely essential to your career and your organization. No matter what your position, others need to be able to believe in and trust your "brand." Rules like "Be discreet," "Self-confidence," and "The world doesn't owe you a living" show you how to develop and nurture this brand, the brand of you. Your brand gives you staying power in a world where reputations can be ruined overnight. It will bring in more business, and push you to the next level at your job. Without it, you'll be left spinning your wheels.

Protect your brand fiercely—it's one of the most powerful assets you have. Reputations are fragile and it's difficult to resurrect them after a serious misstep. Every business functions within a small global community, and people are always watching. A leader's brand must stand for integrity; his actions must consistently build confidence in his brand.

Think about the impact of your behavior on your reputation. Set standards that reflect your values and live up to them.

Self-confidence

Acting with self-confidence makes you more effective. It helps you handle difficult conversations assertively and compassionately. It gives you comfort in the face of uncertainty and keeps you open to learning new ideas. Self-confidence helps you do the things that lead to sustainable business results.

Build your self-confidence by acting in a way that's consistent with your values. *Your values are your deepest beliefs. They never change.* Integrity, optimism, learning, family, winning—these are all values. Many people share some values, but everyone has his or her own unique set. Use yours to build confidence.

Having values puts you in a positive frame of mind. Knowing what your values are will give you the self-confidence to make good choices. Every time you make choices using them, it increases your confidence. This in turn reinforces your values. The reverse is also true. When you behave in a way that contradicts or undermines your values, you feel uncomfortable, and your self-confidence shrinks.

When approaching a decision, we're often so focused on getting a specific result that we sometimes rationalize away our values. Few people sit down and think, "Here are my options—what are my values?" Take a moment and write down the five or six beliefs that matter most to you—the nonnegotiable ones that define who you are. The next time you feel a gnawing in the pit of your stomach over a decision—the sense that you're trying to talk yourself into something—review your list. Make a decision that's consistent with your beliefs. And watch what happens to your self-confidence.

Respect yourself

Where does the heart pump freshly oxygenated blood first? The brain? The lungs? The liver? No. The heart pumps freshly oxygenated blood first to itself. There is natural brilliance to this system. The heart must care for itself before supplying other critical organs or it won't be able to serve the other parts of the body. This system holds true in the workplace too. Respect yourself first. You cannot serve others unless you take care of yourself. Let others know in clear, unambiguous terms that you won't tolerate disrespect from them.

A manager in a global marketing company once worked for six months to generate a report for her boss that represented her best thinking and that of her colleagues. At the meeting to present the report, her boss thought it was more important to clip his fingernails than to look at her while she was speaking. Clip, clip. She stopped the presentation and said, "This seems like a bad time for you. Can we set up a better time?" While remaining polite, she let him know in the most direct way possible that she really needed his full attention and input. He got the message—he stopped clipping and focused on what she had to say. Be direct and dignified and people will respond in kind.

If you don't respect yourself, no one else will. When you do, others take it as a sign that you deserve it.

Treat others with respect

When a man snaps his fingers for a waiter, does he receive better service or worse? Worse, of course. The same holds true in business. We all want to be respected, but in order to receive respect, you have to give respect. Respect the people around you. You'll get more things done, and done well, if you do. Here are some ways to show respect in the workplace:

- Be on time.
- Don't interrupt.

- Don't waste other people's time.
- Don't read your e-mail or take phone calls while someone is talking to you.
- Look people in the eye.
- Acknowledge others when you see them.
- Be prepared when you're asked to report.

Genuine respect is based on a belief that the other person's thoughts and time have value. Approaching people in this way elevates you, as well.

Surround yourself with ethical people

The people around you play a key role in how you think and act. They can challenge you to be your best, or they can undermine or dilute your standards. Surround yourself with people who share your values. Join only companies and groups that share your values. When you face complicated questions ask for advice from the people you've chosen to have in your life, and listen.

If you are assigned to work with colleagues who don't share your ethical standards, minimize your time with them. They can damage your productivity and promotability. Stay focused on the work at hand. Never lower your standards to theirs. If they're doing something illegal, discuss it with your supervisor. If it goes on too long, consider looking for a new team or company.

Set a good example

Many parents have said, "Do as I say, not as I do." But this is a losing strategy, at home and at work. Your actions tell your team what is acceptable, not just your words. If you are always late for meetings, you build a team culture where lateness is allowed. If you frequently lose your temper and yell at others, those behaviors will become the norm. But if you work hard, respect company resources, and stay positive, you build a team environment where good behavior is expected. Catchy sayings on coffee mugs won't do it. Actions will.

Make a list of the things your direct reports do that concern you most. Review the list and ask yourself, "What kind of example do I set"? If you see a disconnect between your actions and your words, commit to doing things the way you want them done.

When you purposefully set the standard you want with your actions, you become a better manager. You are able to handle things more effectively and get more done. A piano teacher's technique is never better than when he's demonstrating good technique for his students. Be the best on your team by exhibiting the behaviors you want to see from everyone.

Always act ethically

Never lie, cheat, or steal. Don't violate company policy or break the law. Submit only legitimate business expenses on your expense reports. Work hard whenever you are "on the clock." Make any personal calls and send any personal packages on your own time and your own dime.

Behave ethically, and make sure people know you do. Doing so will help to build your credibility. When faced with an ethical dilemma, let colleagues know about it, and know your decision. Sharing with them in a collegial way will help let people know who you are.

Keep in mind, however, there's a difference between righteousness and self-righteousness. Everyone missteps at times. Hold to your standards, but avoid being overly critical or judgmental.

Be discreet

Indiscretion in the office is a common occurrence, but it's always a bad idea. Even if it doesn't get you in hot water directly, it'll most likely have a negative effect on people's perception of you. Use the following guidelines to avoid falling into this trap, however tempting it may be.

AVOID GOSSIP

Don't engage in speculation about the personal or work-related concerns of people in the office. It's highly unprofessional.

DON'T MALIGN THE LEADERSHIP OR THEIR POLICIES

Everyone needs to let off a little steam sometimes. But don't do this with colleagues at happy hour or as a bonding exercise on business trips. And never indulge in maligning your company with your direct reports. If you need to vent, talk to a friend outside the office (but put a time limit on it if you value the friendship). If you disagree with something and you'd like to voice your thoughts, talk to your boss face to face.

HANDLE CONFIDENCES WITH CARE

When someone asks, "Can I tell you something in confidence?" don't automatically say yes. Take the time to make a judgment. Most people are so seduced by the notion of knowing something other people don't know that they agree too quickly. It's not always a good idea. Ask what it's about in general terms. If the subject makes you uncomfortable at all, simply say, "I think I'd rather be in the dark on this one." Always let people know up front that if something they tell you puts the company or another person at risk, you can't keep the confidence. But if you agree to let the person confide in you and the information doesn't harm anyone, honor your word.

The world doesn't owe you a living

No one owes you a salary, a bonus, or benefits. There are many people who'd like to have your job. Your relationship with your employer is based solely on the value you create. Your edge comes in adding more value than other people.

Sometimes, after you've been with the organization a while, you may start to think, "No one else can do what I can do; I know too much about the organization. They owe me for so many years of good service." You might think you're entitled to expense meals with friends or to use the company car service for personal business. Such a sense of entitlement leads to arrogance and insensitivity, which can lead to corrupt or inappropriate actions. It lies at the heart of all corporate scandals—people think they are owed more than they are getting paid.

If you're not satisfied with your salary and you think you can get a better package somewhere else, leave your job. Don't let a sense of entitlement tempt you to lower your standards. The chance to add value in an organization is a privilege. We're all fortunate to have it. Be grateful for it, and make the most of it.

Invest in Relationships

Strong relationships are the foundation of business, and life. To be successful and live a happy, purposeful life, you need help from others. No one can do it alone. Family, friends, colleagues, employers, customers—all have the potential to enrich your life. The lessons in this section, such as "Face time counts," "Set up a 'relationships radar screen,'" and "What goes around comes around," equip you with the foundation to start, or strengthen, your base of relationships. Over time, you may be amazed at how your contacts bolster your career. Small gestures—like checking in with an old boss to say hello, or congratulating a coworker—may seem unimportant at the time. But you will be surprised how often these gestures can result in personal and professional advancement. On the flip side, not reaching out to others can weaken your network of contacts, and result in career stagnation. Building and maintaining these relationships is not easy. It requires time, energy, and focus in a fast-moving, distraction-filled world. But it is time well spent.

Investing in relationships is like investing money—you get a return from your investment. That return can take many forms—it can result in a business advantage or simply a good feeling. Smart people, in establishing an investment strategy, make decisions based their objectives. Adopt a "relationship strategy" at work following the same concept. Your time and energy are finite assets. Spend them wisely on relationships that challenge you to grow, and that enhance your career and quality of life.

Business friendship with contacts outside the office are an important part of the strategy. But don't forget your team. People leave bad or inattentive bosses. As a manager, your work life is only as good as your team. The better the people that you attract and keep, the easier and more fun your job is.

Reach out to people consistently. Bring them around you in times of need and celebration. Value them genuinely. Invest in them strategically.

Set up a "relationships radar screen"

Professional salespeople do this, but it is a valuable practice for anyone in business. A radar screen lets you know
where others stand in relation to you. When you meet
someone who might further your goals or teach you something, get their contact information and put it in an elec-
tronic file. Then work to establish a relationship with
them. Don't act disingenuously—if you don't like or respect the person, let the connection go.

Use your radar screen to make sure you stay in touch.
Radar takes a 360-degree sweep every ten seconds. Make

your sweep by focusing on these relationships periodically—once a week, once a month, or once every few months, depending on the relationship. Use a system to remind you who you haven't spoken to recently. Call them, e-mail them, or get together if you have the time. If you come across information that you think would be useful to them (like a magazine article or a book), send it along with a short note. All it needs to say is "Thought you might find this interesting. Hope all is well." Stay alert for opportunities to help them with their goals. Reach out if you hear of a significant success or particular challenge to offer congratulations or support.

Your key relationships deserve your consistent attention. Strong, diverse business friendships are an asset that makes you more valuable to your company and more desirable as a prospective employee. They also improve the quality of your life.

What goes around comes around

When you give generously in relationships, you create an energy that brings good things back to you. Here's a four-point plan:

- When making a business contact, don't start with your hand out. Look for ways to help the other person first. Providing support as they develop clients or change jobs is a perfect opportunity.
- Pay attention to detail. Keep track of people's birthdays, wedding dates, spouses' and children's names. Send

cards and always send regards along to family members by name. (Store this information in your computer, PDA, or Rolodex. On the first of every month, look to see what events are coming up.)

• Go the extra mile. Do special things that people will remember. If a key customer or special colleague mentions he's taking his wife to dinner at a special restaurant for her birthday, find out which one and arrange to have the waiter offer them a drink on you. It's not expensive, but it's thoughtful.

• Make a sincere gesture when it makes sense to do so. If the person loves football and you have season tickets, offer him your seats. Send him your parking pass and the directions. Such a thoughtful gesture won't be forgotten.

Remember: friends do business with friends. Colleagues support colleagues. Make a sincere effort among your circle of business friends and in return they'll make your business and your life richer.

Do breakfast

Breakfast is the new lunch. It's much easier for people to be out of the office for a breakfast appointment. They're still fresh and energized. Meals are usually shorter. The morning's news provides topics to discuss. It's a great way to make business contacts. There's a natural ending to breakfast, while lunch can drag on, with dessert, coffee, etc. And a heavy lunch can make for a sluggish afternoon.

Do breakfast with someone on your "relationships

radar screen" regularly. It's an efficient way to stay connected. It leaves you the whole day to follow up on things you may have discussed. You'll thank yourself for the rest of the day.

Face time counts

Never underestimate the importance of face time. A CEO of a Fortune 500 company walks through his entire U.S. headquarters in December each year to wish two thousand employees a happy holiday in person. He has a piece of candy at every stop (he claims to put on ten pounds at Christmas time every year). He wants to thank them face to face. He knows that during the year he will have to e-mail to the entire group asking for their support, and it helps if they see him as a real person.

Spend 10 percent of *your* time each day connecting with

the people in your operating group. Listen to what they're thinking and feeling, and if you can, try to make them feel good. It can involve a significant investment of time, but the payoff is huge.

The same holds true outside of work. When someone on your team invites you to a wedding, bar mitzvah, or funeral, try to show up. There are a million reasons not to go, but an even more important reason to go, when you can: it shows respect. If you cannot attend, express your regret, send a handwritten note and, if appropriate, a gift. If someone is hospitalized, go in person. They will appreciate it, and you will have reaffirmed their importance in your life. These actions strengthen valuable relationships and build loyalty. It's the right thing to do.

Picking your team is 90 percent of the battle

Just like on the playground at school, picking your team is 90 percent of the battle. Finding the right fit saves time and money down the road—in training, rework, or tackling low productivity. Don't rush this process. The price tag is too high.

Know what skills and experience the job requires. Work with the human resources department to understand the jobs in your area and what kinds of candidates will succeed. If HR can't help you, ask the people doing the job now what skills they think someone will need. Interview people who appear to have these skills.

Call references personally if you have time, and ask HR to check credentials. Alarmingly, some studies show that up to 34 percent of résumés contain false or misleading information. If you find a discrepancy, give the candidate a chance to respond. It could be a record-keeping mistake. But if it's not, don't hire them.

When you're interviewing candidates, ask them to talk about how their experience or education relates to the skills your work requires. Meet with candidates at least twice to be sure they give a consistent response and have a clear picture of the job.

Describe the work and the organization completely and honestly. Often candidates will self-select out of a job if they know it's a bad fit. If your HR department does the hiring for you, insist on partnering in the process. You're the one who will pay the price for a misfire.

Note: Make sure you're working within the bounds of employment law. Ask your lawyer or HR department to help with this—they should be able to assist you.

Help your team members get ahead

A great team makes your life a lot easier. How do you attract bright, hard-working people with great attitudes? By creating opportunity. The go-getters look to the future. Get a reputation as a manager whose people move up and you'll find this kind of employee knocking on your door.

Train and develop your team. Make sure they're confident with the work you're asking them to do. Talk with new team members on their first day and share what you think makes someone promotable. Encourage them to think about where they'd like their careers to go in the future. Let them know you'll work with them to develop the skills and experience they'll need by providing opportunities for training, coaching, and special projects. And when they achieve, praise them publicly. Make sure other decision-makers know about their accomplishments.

There's one downside risk. If you have someone who's ready to be promoted, she knows it. If you don't have a spot for her, she'll start looking elsewhere or someone will come along and cherry-pick her. Work with your boss to identify a special assignment or project that keeps that person with the organization until an opportunity opens up. Look for special initiatives in the business plan and talk with the right people to get your person involved.

You may be thinking, "Why do I want people who just want to move on?" Because they're more talented and motivated than people who are satisfied to find a job and stay in it. You'll consistently have higher-quality people on your team who bring better results with less effort.

Coach your team all day long

Coaching team members makes your job easier in two ways: it improves the quality of their work and, as a result, your unit's financial performance. It is, however, a substantial investment of time so invest it carefully. Initiate coaching relationships with everyone who reports directly to you. Stick with the ones who show you genuine effort and improved performance.

Be clear about what coaching is and isn't. People think it means giving feedback. Giving feedback is only part of it. They think it happens in a coaching "session"—sometimes it does, but much of it happens in a series of moments over time. Many coaches think it's their job to "fix" the other person. In fact, it's the person being coached who's responsible for the coaching's success. If people show you that they're not open to change, don't continue the relationship. It's not a good use of time for either of you.

Start coaching relationships with a one-on-one meeting. Ask the person to make one list of what he does well and another of what he wishes he did better. Then invite him to choose three things to work on (they can come from either list). Next have him set a goal connected to each one, something like "This month, I'll present for my team at the weekly department meetings." Remind him of what he does well and how it can help him. For example, "You're so well organized. How can you use your organization skills to be a better presenter?" Let him know that you think he can do it. It's a powerful inspiration to feel that someone else believes in you. Never lie, only say it if you believe it. Schedule time to touch base to see how it went.

As you see the person work every day, watch for chances to congratulate him on progress. If you see him struggle with something, ask him privately if he needs any help, or ideas on how he could've handled it better.

True coaching elicits excellence. You know you're doing it right when the other person takes control of the work and starts to drive it, when *he* comes to *you* and asks for coaching instead of *you* approaching *him*.

Don't let employees get bored

Have you ever felt totally confident in a job? Faced every type of challenge that had come along? Had every day be pretty much the same, with few challenges? If you're like most people, it felt great for about a month before becoming boring. The mind is like a muscle. If you don't exercise it, it starts to atrophy. Motivated people need to be challenged.

When a team member handles the work you're asking of her too easily, challenge her or give her a new assignment. Overconfidence kills motivation, especially for top performers. Assign them to do research about a new customer, or improve a process. Talk with them about their career goals and find a project that advances their goals while improving your department's performance.

Keeping employees motivated isn't a one-size-fits-all proposition. You need to observe each person's comfort with his current work and be familiar with his individual goals to keep each one operating at peak performance. It's a balance. Don't overwhelm them, but don't let them stagnate either. Top performers are always hungry for new experiences.

Recognize the doers

A national survey asked employees and their supervisors at multiple companies to rank what best motivated the employees. The supervisors thought the employees cared most about "good wages." But the employees themselves said that "full appreciation for work being done" was the top motivator. "Good wages" ranked fifth. This is a common misperception. Managers often don't understand the power of recognizing an employee's contribution.

As a manager, do it often and do it publicly—the more

public, the better. It doesn't need to be elaborate. Here are three quick ways to recognize people.

- *Thanks* This is appropriate when someone has done something extra—helped a colleague get a report out or stayed late to make a deadline. "Thank you" says, "I know you went above and beyond the call of duty and I appreciate that."
- *Congratulations* Offer congratulations when someone finishes a big project or lands an account or does something that's usually hard for him or her. "Congratulations" says, "You've accomplished something special. You deserve to feel proud."
- *Great work* Whenever someone's day-to-day work is excellent, say so. "Great work today, Liz." This says, "I recognize the quality of the work you do every day." Offer this only when the work *has* been great. People know when they haven't done their best, and so do you.

Every time you get the chance, point out things you want your team to do more of. The productivity payback is tremendous. And don't forget to recognize the achievements of your colleagues and your boss. They like to be recognized too.

Satisfied employees = loyal customers = bigger profits

Research shows an important chain reaction in service companies. Satisfied employees create loyal customers who in turn become apostles for your business. These apostles create new customers, who drive up profits.* When that same great service makes your new customer a return customer, the profit margin grows even more. The correlation is undeniable. What makes employees so satisfied that they can drive profits up? It's feeling that they do

---

* James L. Heskett et al., "Putting the Service-Profit Chain to Work" (*Harvard Business Review*, March-April 1994, pp. 164–74, Volume 72, Issue 2).

good work and are treated with respect by their companies and managers.

Here's just one initiative that a major-airline CEO used to put this principle to work: He created a crisis fund, wherein he would match employees' contributions from his own salary. The money was used to help crew members in crisis—for instance if an employee's house burned down. He also emphasized that, when on the job, each crew member's needs had to be taken care of first, so that they could take proper care of the customer. For example, during a rainstorm when flights are delayed, the crew routinely stays late and helps passengers when they arrive. It's mandatory overtime. In this company the manager was encouraged to buy the crew pizza and let them rest in the break room until the planes arrived—even though they were on the clock—to make sure the team was ready to help the passengers. Their high job satisfaction and self-respect motivated them to give great service. In the end, the extremely high customer loyalty translated into increased business, which pays off all the way down the line to the shareholder.

Don't pass up this potential advantage. A surprising amount of companies do.

To be a superstar, you have to stop being a star

If you score every one of your team's eighty points in a basketball game and the other team scores eighty-four, you've still lost. Beyond that, you were taking all the shots, which demoralizes the rest of your team and makes them lose interest in helping you make your basket.

Great players bring the whole team up. They provide leadership. They challenge other players to work hard, cheer for their successes, and encourage them to keep working when things aren't going well. Watch true superstars play. You see them call out to other players throughout the game. They pass off when they don't have a shot and they protect the person who does. They believe in their teammates, and their faith raises everyone's level of play. When the spotlight shines on them, they bring other players into the light and make sure their contributions don't get overshadowed. And, of course, they play a great game themselves.

Everyone wants to advance his career. But if your goals are too self-centered, you'll never get the support you need to get results. Stay focused on working with your team to deliver something great for the customer. That's the path to true superstardom.

No one is irreplaceable

Often managers will get into a hostage situation with a very talented employee. The manager feels the person is too valuable to lose so he compromises his standards. The employee may become openly antagonistic and demanding. She'll start to infect the rest of the team. The more she gets away with, the more disdainful she becomes, the more disgruntled the team gets. It's an expensive and damaging cycle.

Here's how a great leader handled a situation like this. An elite group was assembled to design a critical initiative.

Management chose a team leader, but then switched course and gave the position to a different person against the team's wishes. The team members were angry and flaunted the fact that they were updating their résumés. The new leader met with them on his first day. They expected him to beg them to stay. But that's not what happened. Firmly, but matter-of-factly, he told them all that if they planned to quit, he'd like them to quit that day. If they came in the next day, he expected them to be committed to the project and table the attitude. He also let them know he'd like them to stay, but on the conditions he had described—complete commitment, no attitude. Jarred by the reality that they weren't irreplaceable, every team member stayed, with a new attitude.

No one is so valuable they can't be replaced. Don't be held hostage. Let people know you value them, but will make a change if you need to. It's better for them and you.

You can't force someone to be productive

Often managers fall into the trap of thinking it's their job to make an unproductive person productive. That's a fallacy. As a manager you can invite people to be productive, establish standards, and support them while they try. But you can never make someone productive if they don't want to be. It's wasted energy and it drags down everyone around you. Employees have to have the will to change. This person typically does the minimum, enough to simply "get by." Meanwhile you're burning 15 percent of your time trying to get her up to the performance standard.

Carefully lay the foundation for accountability (see page 108, "Accountability begins at the beginning") and set a time frame for improvement. If the person's performance doesn't meet the level you put in place, end the relationship.

To say the same thing over and over again and expect a different response will only bring frustration. If you have a colleague or employee who never delivers on a promise, stop waiting for him to do it. If the person works for you, take the appropriate action. If he's a peer, minimize your dependence on him. You jeopardize your own performance by expecting others to behave differently than they have in the past.

Seek out the "energy generators"

The people around you dramatically affect your energy, your productivity, and your capacity to learn. Use this to your advantage.

Smart, motivated, productive people are like a jolt of electricity. They give you a boost. They make you feel better about yourself, and perform better. They make work more fun. By contrast, negative and cynical people are an energy siphon. You go into a meeting room with them and you can feel the life getting sucked right out of you. You feel tired and bored.

Spend as much time as possible with energy generators. When building a team, select people who bring vigor to the table. They will fuel you and each other. They'll get more done, better, with less effort from you. Minimize the time you spend with energy-drainers. When you replay that day's tape, make sure you didn't give the day away to these people.

Surrounding yourself with energy generators is the highest form of self-respect. More than any other change you can make on your own, this will transform your work life.

Respect the gatekeepers

A gatekeeper is someone, often an administrative assistant, who manages access to an important person. Executives partner with them in an important way and come to rely on their judgment and perceptions. Assistants help executives make key decisions about scheduling and day-to-day priorities. Often they decide who will get the boss's time and who won't. Frequently executives ask their administrative assistant for a candid frontline perspective or for a sense of the organization's mood. Never underestimate this person's importance. It's outdated to think they're coffee-getters.

Here's a classic example of old-school thinking. An executive wanted to reach the CEO. He continued to press the CEO's executive assistant to get the CEO's attention for him, telling her it was very important. But he wouldn't tell her what it was about. He didn't think the assistant could understand what he was asking. The assistant broke in on the CEO. When the CEO was finally able to respond, he discovered that the matter wasn't truly urgent and the assistant could've handled it on her own. Both the CEO and the assistant were furious and it strained the executive's relationship with both of them.

Executive assistants are smart, accomplished professionals. They deserve your respect, and they know when they're not getting it.

Gain Perspective

In results-driven environments, gaining perspective is hard. It's easy to become so driven by emptying your in-box that you stop taking the time to determine what really matters in life. Urgency becomes mania and your productivity actually goes down. Stress in the workplace is a huge problem. If you're stressed all the time, chances are you're not doing your job as well as you can. Rules like "Know when to take a deep breath," "Make room for all parts of your life," and "Setbacks make us stronger" will help you to release tension and stay focused. Some people view taking time for yourself to unwind as self-indulgent. But in reality, it's a must, for your long-term health as well as for your career.

When all you can see is your in-box, you have a skewed perspective. The trick is to find a way to gain a more valid perspective, to be able to see how your actions, behavior, and thinking affect your outlook, your personal relationships, and your private life. Sometimes you have to get to a higher ground to see this. It's like climbing a mountain to see the valley below. When you get there, the air is fresh and the view is expansive. Such a view can help to regenerate you.

Gaining perspective is a pursuit, not an event. Work to achieve perspective on the world and yourself. Look for experiences that stretch your worldview. It will give you balance, replenish your spirit, and make you more of a friend to yourself and more valuable to your organization.

Know what you want

Remove the mystery from getting what you want. Write down your goals and a course of action to achieve them. It clarifies your thinking and makes you more accountable to yourself.

Use this modified business planning exercise. Get a stack of five-by-seven-inch index cards and sit at a large table. On each card, write down one thing you want to have in your life five years from now. Do you want to be spending time with your kids? Taking exotic vacations? Do you plan on an early retirement? Write them all down—*one per card*. Take an exhaustive inventory—don't limit yourself. If you're married, you might want to do this exercise with your spouse.

Next, in the upper righthand corner, write a number between one and six on each card—six for the most important, one for the least important. Pull out the fives and sixes and lay them out in front of you. Read them over. Now pick the most important three. From those three, choose one that is nonnegotiable, that you would give up everything else to have. Keep this card on top.

On the front of each of the three most important cards, write one sentence that describes what success in this goal looks like. On the back write four steps you will take this year to move toward that vision of success. These key goals, your definition of success, and the action steps become the base of your personal action plan. Transfer them to a one-page document. Always keep it with you. Review and adjust it each year.

Your goals and priorities will change over time. Always keep your current goals on a single sheet of paper with you. It demystifies the future, and will keep you on track and help you get what you want.

Setbacks make us stronger

When I was twenty-five years old I was elected to the New York State Assembly. One great perk of sitting in the legislature was a set of special license plates that show you are a member. I loved those license plates. Two years later, running for reelection in 1974, I was one of many swept out of office with the back end of the Watergate broom. I held on to my license plates until the last possible moment, the day they *had* to be turned in. They'd become a symbol of who I was. Surrendering those plates represented my loss of status in the community. I was filled with self-doubt.

At twenty-seven years old, I had learned one of life's most important lessons. We are not what we do. We are much more than that. Each of us has a unique combination of beliefs, values, experiences, knowledge, and potential. I'm a loving husband, a deeply committed parent, a good friend, and a hard-working professional who strives to do the right thing. I love nature and gardening. That is more than a set of vanity tags. They are things that no one can take away.

Setbacks happen, but we can survive them. I worked hard to learn everything I could from this event. It forced me to think about who I was and what I had to offer—my enduring, inherent value. That made me stronger and, ultimately, happier. In the end, I learned to define myself and not let others do it for me. And I'm grateful for that.

Avoid arrogance—nobody does it alone

Arrogance can damage your relationships with those around you. It's the learning equivalent of blinders. The truth is, we've been getting help directly or indirectly from people our whole lives, no matter how independent we perceive ourselves to be. Avoid thinking you're better than everyone else. Don't let yourself fall into that trap.

Many people throughout the organization do things for you each day—often, things you don't do well. Now, think of the rest of the people who've supported you throughout your life and career: your parents, the teachers who helped you to see and achieve your potential, the bosses who took a chance and gave you that stretch assignment. They're all part of your success. No one does it alone.

Keep in mind how much you depend on other people in your organization. Thank them often. You can't do it without them.

Admit your limitations

A CEO of a publicly traded company once said his great strength was his ability to define a vision for the organization's future and energize people about that vision. What were his weaknesses? he was asked. He threw back his head and laughed. He was terrible at detail-oriented planning; in fact, he detested it. He said that throughout his career he always made sure that his team included someone who excelled in this area.

CEOs, executives, and managers all have limitations. An exceptional professional knows her weaknesses and makes intelligent accommodations for them. This demonstrates two things. She's honest with herself and others, and she has enough confidence to admit she doesn't excel at everything.

We all have different talents and abilities. We also all have limitations. That's the real world. Know your strengths and your weaknesses. This will allow you to leverage your strong points, improve areas where you're weak, and get appropriate support from others on your team.

Don't waste energy trying to make others think you know it all. They don't buy it. It's okay to be human.

Know when to take a deep breath

Tight deadlines, rising client expectations, and internal turf battles all contribute to high-pressure days. Get to a higher ground on these days so you have a clear view of what's happening in front of you.

When you feel assaulted, defensive, or angry, don't implode in a tantrum. This is a self-inflicted wound and it can be a career-killer. Here's a red flag: If you catch yourself thinking "I don't need this job. Nothing's worth this," step back. You may be right, but you'll never make a sound decision in that state of mind. Breathe deeply. Promise yourself that you'll think about it after things have calmed down.

Then:

Remember what you're trying to accomplish and focus on solutions.

Keep others around you feeling positive by helping them to handle their challenges.

If possible, help people to laugh—it's a great way to diffuse tension.

Ask yourself: Will whatever I'm upset about matter in six months? Or six weeks?

Remember that it's a big world out there. It will keep spinning even if you make a mistake.

On these days, never:

Blame poor performance on others.

Yell at a colleague or someone on your team.

Put your feelings in writing, such as an e-mail.

Tell a colleague that you'll quit if this kind of thing keeps up.

Make impulsive decisions.

What might seem like an emergency right now is, over the course of a lifetime, only a moment. Don't do something in that moment that could damage your career. Instead, stand out as a person who keeps a clear head and a healthy perspective.

Make room for all parts of your life

Success within any organization requires a high level of confidence, stability, and endurance. These three characteristics will help put you in a place where you can take risks and do the hard work required to get the job done right. But to stay on top of your game, you must recharge your batteries during the time you spend outside of work.

Schedule time for the people you love: your spouse, friends, parents, or children. Protect that time. Your deepest personal relationships help to refuel you. They challenge you to remember who you are and what you value. They hold you accountable and keep you honest.

Don't neglect yourself, either. Spend time in your garden, your kitchen, or the library—whatever reenergizes you. Know what activities recharge you, and schedule them. This is critical. To ignore this is like saying you're too busy to sleep. Sooner or later you'll be too exhausted to get anything done. Invest time in your health. Work out, eat right, get enough sleep, and consult with physicians when you need them. Self-care is a practical investment in your success and ultimate happiness.

Volunteer

Volunteering broadens your perspective, connects you with other action-oriented people, builds your skills, and improves the community. It's good for you in many ways that go beyond simply feeling good about yourself. How can you identify a worthwhile volunteering opportunity? It should offer you the chance to develop new skills, have a mission that's important to you, or give you an opportunity to build relationships.

Take your role seriously and approach it professionally. Do as much as time allows—you'll make the strongest contribution and learn the most. Prepare for meetings. Build trust and credibility by delivering results. Help the organization achieve its goals.

List the skills you can practice at volunteer gatherings, such as meeting management or public speaking. Seek situations that challenge you to use them. Volunteering lets you improve your skills on someone else's nickel. Make the most of it.

Volunteering exposes you to things you don't see in your day job. It expands your social circle and makes you a more interesting person. Do the right thing for the right reasons and volunteering can be a genuinely valuable experience for you and the community.

Get comfortable with not knowing

Business involves constantly facing new situations, complicated problems, and questions that simply have no answer. The uncertainty can drive you crazy unless you accept the fact that the business world isn't always knowable. Instead of black and white, there's a lot of gray. Things can seem fuzzy in the gray area. But you have to learn to be comfortable with this because it's not going to change.

The higher up you go in an organization, the more you have to deal with gray areas inherent in decisions with broad implications. Answers don't come quickly and judgments often must be made without all the necessary facts. Leaders must live with ambiguity. They have to trust that whatever happens, they can handle it. They need to learn to ask for help when they need it. It's part of the job.

The important thing is to face uncertainty head on. It's better to say, "I don't know" or "I'm having trouble defining this problem" than to pretend things are clear. Take a deep breath. Get all the information you can. Ask for help when you need it. And use your best judgment. Then trust in your judgment—remember, making a decision one way or the other is far better than making no decision.

Nothing or nobody can affect you negatively

A man once founded a company from nothing and built it into a major division of a Fortune 100 company. Through many challenging transitions, he never lost his focus. What gave him the confidence to keep pushing when many people would have quit? Years of mental conditioning.

He built his attitude about success brick by brick. He knew there would be detractors, so he taught himself how not to take it personally. He knew there would be distractions and detours, so he developed his concentration. He embraced a phrase to express his philosophy: "Nothing or nobody can affect me negatively."

His philosophy was about personal power. He could choose how to view life; others couldn't alter his opinion of himself unless he let them. He chose not to let them. *He* defined *his* life. He controlled his destiny.

You have the same choice and the same power. You can choose not to let others derail you. Make a choice right now to do this going forward. It takes conditioning and commitment—this man didn't just wake up one day with the inner strength and perspective to accomplish all he did. He worked at it. You have to as well.

Write the phrase "Nothing or nobody can affect me negatively" on a piece of paper. Put it somewhere near your desk where you can see it. Let it remind you of your personal power when someone thoughtlessly demeans you or the pressure of a deadline is weighing on you like a ton of paper. Always keep a positive attitude.

The real power of fundamentals is that by working hard at them you gain the power to control your own destiny. That's my hope for you.

Stuart R. Levine is chairman and CEO of Stuart Levine & Associates LLC, an international consulting and leadership training company that helps leaders to get it right by focusing on the discipline of fundamentals and building an organization's confidence to achieve results.

Among its clients are Microsoft, Cablevision, Symbol Technologies, Harmon Associates Division of Georgia-Pacific Corporation, Vytra Health Plans, the Social Security Administration, Thomas Register, and many others. As former CEO of Dale Carnegie & Associates, Inc., Mr.

Levine received the 1995 Entrepreneur of the Year Award in the category of leadership by Ernst & Young and *Inc.* magazine. He received the 1999 Innovator of the Year Award from PricewaterhouseCoopers, for his Techno-Bridge™ leadership training program designed for technology professionals.

He is coauthor of the international bestseller *The Leader in You*, published in over twenty-two languages. He is a contributing author of *Management 21C*, recognized by Amazon.com in England as the Best Business and Finance Book of 1999. He has been profiled in the *New York Times*, the *Los Angeles Times*, and *USA Today*, and has appeared on CNN, CNBC, and PBS, as well as hundreds of local television and radio shows.

Levine serves as the lead director for Gentiva Health Services. He additionally serves as a director of North Shore–Long Island Jewish Health System, the American College of Physicians–American Society of Internal Medicine Foundation, and the Nature Conservancy. He is former chairman of Dowling College as well as a former member of the New York State Assembly.

He lives on Long Island, New York, with his wife, Harriet, and their two children, Jesse and Elizabeth.